Rotisserie Chicken Grilling

MIKE VROBEL

Other Books by Mike Vrobel

Rotisserie Grilling

Version 1.02

Copyright © 2015 Mike Vrobel

Photographs copyright © 2015 Mike Vrobel

All rights reserved.

Copyright laws and international treaties protect this work.

Product names, brands, and other trademarks referred to within this book are the property of their respective trademark holders. No association between the author and any trademark holder is expressed or implied. Use of a term in this book should not be regarded as affecting the validity of any trademark, registered trademark, or service mark.

ISBN: 0985512539

- About Rotisserie Chicken ... 1
  - Why Rotisserie Chicken? ... 2
  - Seven Steps to Rotisserie Chicken ... 4
  - Carving the Bird ... 12
  - Cooking Times ... 15
  - Seasoning ... 17
  - Is It Done? (The Science of Cooking Chicken) ... 24
  - Charcoal or Gas? ... 28
  - Equipment ... 33
  - FAQ ... 38
- Recipes ... 46
  - The Basics ... 47
  - Brines, Wet and Dry ... 60
  - Grocery Store Seasonings ... 75
  - Spice Rubs ... 87
  - Barbecued Birds ... 99
  - Liquored Up ... 115
  - Mediterranean Herb Pastes ... 130
  - Asian Birds ... 142
  - Busy Busy Birds ... 158
  - Potatoes in the Pan ... 176
  - Leftovers ... 191
- About the Author ... 209
- Bibliography and Suggested Reading ... 211

Thank you, Diane. Your love and support makes me who I am.

Thank you, Ben, Natalie, and Tim, for putting up with dad cooking all the chicken. (So much chicken!)

Thank you to the rest of my family. I wouldn't be here without all the love and support you've given me.

This book is built on the shoulders of all those who went before me, and it wouldn't be here without their inspiration. To the world of food — writers, photographers, chefs, home cooks, farmers, ranchers, butchers, market goers, grillers and grill makers. Thank you all.

ABOUT ROTISSERIE CHICKEN

Why Rotisserie Chicken?

Rotisserie Chicken made me a cookbook author.

Roast chicken is my holy grail of cooking. It's simple, but it's not easy. I have tried every roast chicken technique. From high heat in the oven to low and slow on the barbecue; from sealed in a cast iron pot to grilled on a beer can. Some of these techniques were good, some were only OK, but none of them made me stop looking for a better way to cook a chicken.

Then I cooked a rotisserie chicken on my kettle grill. It looked fantastic — crackling brown skin over juicy meat. When I bit into a drumstick, the clouds parted and a shaft of sunlight burst through. A voice boomed out from the heavens: "This is the one true chicken."

Rotisserie chicken became an obsession, and I turned in to a rotisserie fanatic. Rotisserie recipes were hard to find back then, so I started tinkering. I tried different things, finding out what worked and what didn't. Later on, after I started a food blog, I shared some of my rotisserie recipes — and that's when my traffic took off.

Inspired, I wrote my first cookbook, Rotisserie Grilling. When I finished, I had a problem — too many chicken recipes. I needed space for beef and pork, turkey and lamb. I had to cut chicken recipes, including some favorites that I didn't want to leave out.

Those recipes kept bouncing around in my head, trying to get out… and this book is their outlet. I hope you enjoy rotisserie chicken as much as I do, because I've got a bunch of ideas to share.
Here's the secret about this book — rotisserie chicken is simple. All the recipes use one cooking technique, high heat rotisserie roasting. That technique, in one sentence:

Set the grill up for cooking on indirect high heat, with a drip pan in the middle of the grill; truss and spit a four pound chicken, start it spinning on the grill, and cook with the lid closed until the chicken reaches 160°F in the deepest part of the breast, about one hour.

Is that it? Are we done here? No, far from it. The first part of the book breaks down that sentence, showing you the details of cooking a rotisserie chicken. And, while cooking technique is key, it is not the only key. The second part of the book is the fun part — all the different flavors you can give to a chicken. I've collected flavor profiles from far and wide, so we can travel the world with our rotisserie chicken.

Are you ready to rotisserie? Let's get started.

SEVEN STEPS TO ROTISSERIE CHICKEN

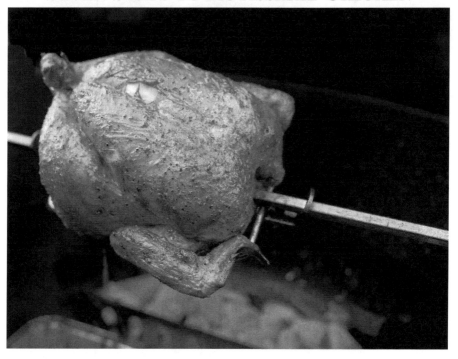

Here is my seven-step program to rotisserie chicken success:

1. Season, truss, and evenly spit a four pound chicken.
2. Set up the grill for indirect high heat, with a drip pan in the middle of the grate.
3. Mount the motor.
4. Plug the spit into the rotisserie bracket, turn on the motor, and start the chicken spinning.
5. Cook with the lid closed until the chicken reaches 160°F in the breast, about an hour.
6. Remove the spit from the grill, remove the chicken from the spit, and cut the trussing twine away from the chicken.
7. Let the chicken rest, then carve and serve!

Let's walk through the rotisserie chicken technique in detail:

Basic Rotisserie Chicken Walkthrough
Equipment
- Grill with rotisserie attachment
- Rotisserie spit with two spit forks
- Trussing twine
- Drip pan

Ingredients
- 1 (4 pound) Chicken
- 1 tablespoon kosher salt
- 1/2 teaspoon fresh ground black pepper

Step 1: Season, truss and spit the chicken
Seasoning
Sprinkle the chicken evenly with salt and pepper, inside and out. Start with the outside of the chicken, seasoning the breast, legs, wings, and back. Sprinkle some of the salt and pepper inside the cavity to season the inside of the bird. If you're feeling adventurous, slide a finger between the skin and the breast, gently working the skin free from the meat. Rub some salt and pepper under the skin, directly on the breast meat.

If possible, season the chicken early — as far ahead as the night before. Let the chicken rest, uncovered, in the refrigerator. The salt acts as a dry brine, working its way deep into the bird, seasoning it all the way through. If you can't salt early, that's OK; seasoning right before cooking still results in a great bird.

Trussing
The chicken needs to be trussed into a tight package before it goes on the spit. Why? If it's not secure, the chicken will flop around as the rotisserie spins and pull itself loose from the spit forks.

Surgeon's knot: I truss chicken with a surgeon's knot — a square knot with an extra twist added to the first tie. That extra twist adds tension to the first tie, holding it tight while I finish the knot with the second tie.

(For my trussing and spitting video, click here: http://youtu.be/MfaTruBmETc)

How to truss: Measure out a piece of butcher's twine about four times the length of the bird. Set the bird on its back, facing away from you.

Find the middle of the piece of twine and loop it over the nub of the neck at the front of the bird. Pull both ends of the string along the sides of the breast, just above the wings, and back to the cavity behind the bird. Tie a surgeon's knot at the cavity, tightening the knot to plump up the breast.

Grab the ends of the strings, and pull them taut. Loop the strings down and under the knobs of the drumsticks. Then, lift up, catching the knobs with the loop of string and pulling the knobs up a little. Start another surgeon's knot, pulling the knobs on the drumsticks across each other. Keep tightening the knot, pushing on the crossed drumsticks, until the legs pull tight against cavity of the bird. Finish the knot and trim the excess string. You're done — the chicken is now trussed in a tight bundle.

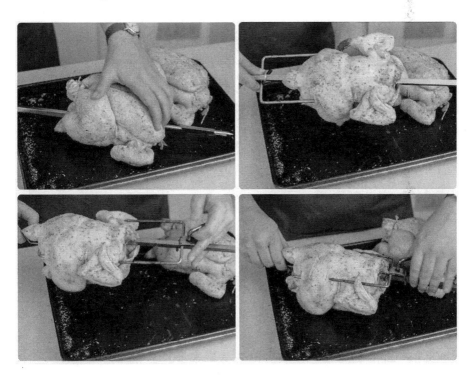

How to spit: Tighten the first spit fork down onto the spit, a little more than halfway to the handle end. Run the spit through the cavity

SEVEN STEPS TO ROTISSERIE CHICKEN 7

of the bird, and sink the fork deep into the chicken's thighs. Slide the other spit fork on to the spit and push the fork into the breast meat just above the chicken's wings. Squeeze the bird between the forks and tighten the second fork onto the spit, locking the bird in place. If the bird is not centered on the spit, loosen the forks, slide the bird to the middle, and then lock the forks down on the spit again.

Step 2: Set the grill for indirect heat

Dripping chicken fat is a grease fire just waiting to happen. To prevent flare-ups, I configure the grill for indirect heat. I bank the coals to the sides of the grill, and put a drip pan in the center of the grate, under the chicken.

Charcoal grill indirect setup

Remove the grill grate and set it aside — we need extra clearance for the chicken to spin. For high heat, light 5 quarts (60 briquettes) of charcoal; for Medium heat, use 3.75 quarts (45 briquettes) of charcoal. (5 quarts is the amount of charcoal needed to fill a large Weber charcoal chimney). The charcoal is ready when it is mostly covered with gray ash, which takes about 20 minutes. Pour the lit charcoal into two even piles on the sides of the charcoal grate. Put the drip pan in the middle of the grate, between the piles. (If your grill has charcoal baskets or rails, use them; they hold the coals on the side of the grill where we want them).

A four pound chicken will finish in about an hour. This is a good thing, because charcoal will burn out and start to lose heat rapidly after an hour of cooking. If the cooking time is longer than an hour, refuel the grill with extra coals. Add the unlit briquettes to the piles of burning charcoal in the grill. For high heat, add 24 unlit briquettes every hour; for medium heat, add 16 briquettes.

Gas Grill indirect setup

Remove the grates from the grill and set them aside — we need extra clearance for the chicken to spin. Preheat the grill for fifteen minutes with all burners on high. Turn off the burners in the middle of the grill, leaving the burners on the edges lit. Put the drip pan on the burner covers in the middle of the grill, over the unlit burner(s). If your gas grill has a dedicated infrared rotisserie burner, light it now.

Most rotisserie chicken is cooked on high heat. With the outer burners on high and an infrared rotisserie burner, the grill should reach 450°F or higher. For medium heat, adjust the burners to get an internal grill temperature of 350°F. (You may have to turn off the infrared burner to get down to medium heat.)

Never Trust a Thermometer
By the way, the thermometer in the lid of your grill may be lying to you. Test your grill's thermometer by setting the grill up for indirect high heat, and then put an oven thermometer in the middle of the grate. If the lid thermometer and the thermometer on the grate don't match, make a note the difference in temperature. That way, you know how much you need to adjust your grill to get the correct temperature. (If they're way off — more than fifty degrees — contact your grill manufacturer and buy a new thermometer for your lid.)

Step 3: Mount the motor
If your grill has a detachable rotisserie mount, like a ring that fits in a kettle grill, put it in place now. Then, slide the motor onto the motor mount, and plug it in. (It always works better when it's plugged in.)

Step 4: Plug the spit into the rotisserie bracket and turn on the motor
Bring the spitted chicken out to the grill. Plug the point of the spit into the rotisserie motor, and set the notch on the spit into the groove on the other side of the grill. Turn on the rotisserie motor and start the chicken spinning. Center the drip pan under the chicken, close the lid, and keep it closed as much as possible.

Step 5: Cook with the lid closed until the chicken reaches 160°F in the breast, about an hour

How long will the chicken take? That depends on a lot of variables — the heat of the fire, the volume of the grill, the weather, the size of the chicken. The best way to check doneness is an instant read thermometer. The chicken will read 160°F in the thickest part of the breast, and 170°F or higher in the deepest part of the leg. But, a rough estimate for a four pound chicken is 1 hour at high heat, and 1 hour 15 minutes at medium heat. (See the cooking times chapter for more information on different sizes of birds and cooking times.)

Step 6: Remove the spit from the grill, remove the chicken from the spit, and cut the trussing twine away from the chicken

When the chicken is done, remove the spit from the grill. Wear heat proof gloves to protect your hands and arms— the hot spit is a branding iron. Loosen the spit forks and slide the chicken off of the spit, and then remove the trussing twine from the chicken immediately. (Why immediately? The more the chicken cools, the more it will stick to the spit forks and the trussing twine.)

To remove the chicken from the spit: set the chicken (still on the spit) down on a carving board. Loosen the first spit fork. (Depending on the shape of the spit fork knobs, use a set of pliers or a dinner fork for leverage.) Pull the spit fork free from the chicken and slide it off of the spit. Loosen the fork on the back of the chicken, grab the fork with a pair of tongs, and pull the spit straight back. The spit will slide out of the chicken (and the fork), leaving the chicken sitting on the cutting board. (Think of drawing a sword from its scabbard — that's the effect you want.) Set the spit aside, resting the handle and point on heatproof surfaces. Pull the fork out of the back of the bird. Cut the twine holding the knobs of the drumsticks together, then reach between the legs and cut the twine next to the knot at the cavity. The twine is now loose; gently pull it away from the chicken.

Step 7: Let the chicken rest, then carve and serve

Let the chicken rest for 10 to 15 minutes before carving. The muscle fibers in the chicken are tight from the heat of cooking; if we cut into the bird right away, those tight fibers squeeze juices out of the meat. Resting the chicken lets the muscle fibers relax, so the juices stay in the meat where we want them. After resting, carve the chicken and serve.

Carving the Bird

The key to carving is a sharp knife. I prefer a chef's knife for carving, but any long, sharp knife will work. I've carved chicken with everything from a fancy carving set down to a paring knife. (I don't recommend using a paring knife — it's annoying — but it can get the job done.)

The other key to carving is to avoid cutting through bones. Instead, we'll cut through the joints that hold the bird together.

(Click here for my carving a chicken video: http://youtu.be/Xv-rN0zcHQU)

First, cut the legs away from the chicken. Set the chicken on its backbone, drumsticks pointing towards you. Slice the skin between the leg and the body until you can see where the thigh meets the backbone. Grab the leg and push down to the cutting board, popping the joint and exposing the ball of the thigh bone. Run the knife through that joint and along the backbone, cutting the leg away from the chicken. Lay the leg on the cutting board, skin side down, and cut through the joint that joins the drumstick to the thigh. Repeat with the other leg.

Next, remove the breast meat from the body. Make a horizontal slice just above the wing, all the way to the bone. Then, find the keel bone running along the top of the breast. Slice down one side of the keel bone until you reach the ribcage. Pull the breast meat away from the carcass while slicing with your knife along the curve of ribcage. Keep pulling and slicing to free the breast from the ribs. Set the breast on the cutting board, skin side up, and slice crosswise into half inch thick slices. Repeat with the other breast.

Last, remove the chicken wings. Pull the wing to expose the joint holding the wing to the body, and slice through that joint. Trim off the wingtip, but leave the wingette and the drumette connected. Repeat with the other wing.

You're done! Discard the carcass. (Or, even better, save it for soup — see the chicken stock recipe in the leftovers chapter.)

COOKING TIMES

Weight of Chicken	Heat Level	Estimated Cooking Time
2 pounds (Cornish Hen)	High	40 minutes
3 pounds	High	50 minutes
4 pounds	High	1 hour
4 pounds	Medium	1 hour 15 minutes
5 pounds	Medium	1 hour 30 minutes
6 pounds	Medium	1 hour 45 minutes
8 pounds	Medium	2 hours
10 pounds (Capon)	Medium	2 hours 15 minutes

- High heat is at least 450°F; higher is better
- Medium heat is 350°F

Four pounds is where I switch between high to medium heat. If the chicken is smaller than four pounds, it needs high heat or the skin won't crisp up before the meat is cooked. If the chicken is larger than four pounds, then we have the opposite problem; the skin will burn before the meat cooks through. Four pound birds can go either way — they are the right size for medium or high heat.

I have to get something off my chest.

The cooking time chart is a lie.

Phew, now I feel better.

There is no such thing as precise cooking times for live fire cooking. Maybe my charcoal is running hot today. Maybe your gas grill runs cooler than mine, and your high heat is 475°F, but mine is 625°F. Maybe you have an extra strong infrared rotisserie burner. Maybe it's a windy day, pulling heat out of the grill; maybe the sun is bright and heating up the kettle. Maybe this chicken is plumper than the last one. Maybe I was impatient, kept opening the grill to check on the chicken, and let too much heat escape.

Maybe, maybe, maybe... There are too many variables.

I have a feel for how a grilling session is coming along. I know my grills. I've cooked a lot of rotisserie chicken, and my chicken sense is strong. Most of the time, a four pound chicken cooked over indirect high heat takes one hour, almost exactly on the nose. But...sometimes it is ten minutes fast; sometimes it is ten minutes slow. I start checking the temperature with an instant read thermometer fifteen minutes before I think the bird should finish cooking.

What I'm trying to say is: this timing chart is a guide, not a monument carved in stone. Get to know your grill, trust your experience, and start checking the chicken a little before you think you should.

SEASONING

A simple rotisserie chicken, seasoned with salt and pepper, makes a fabulous dinner. But why stop there? Chicken works with all sorts of different flavors. Let's look at the various ways we can season a chicken.

Salt and Pepper
Quick, effective, and the default seasoning option in western cuisine. Sprinkle the chicken with salt and pepper right before it goes on the grill. Salt brings out the flavor of food, making it taste more like itself. (No matter how big the rush, please don't forget the salt!)

Pepper adds a spicy, floral bite…as long as you use fresh ground pepper. Cracking a peppercorn releases its flavors, but they start to evaporate immediately. Pre-ground pepper is a shadow of fresh ground pepper, straight from the pepper mill.

Brining - dry, wet, and injection
Modern food science has shown that we can improve on "salt the chicken and put it on the grill" by giving salt time to work on the meat.

I used to say: "salt is absorbed through osmosis". And, while that's true, it is not the entire story. Salt does enter the meat through osmosis; if you wait long enough, the salt in the brine will penetrate the meat, seasoning it all the way through. But there's more going on. The salt actually changes the structure of the meat, denaturing the protein, causing the muscle fibers to swell. As the muscle fibers swell, they trap water (and the salt) inside the meat.

Why does this matter? When meat is cooked, those muscle fibers tighten up, squeezing liquid out of the meat; that's why overcooked meat is dry. Brined, swollen muscle fibers hang on to the salt and water, even when they tighten up from cooking. The result? Brined meat is juicier meat.

Dry brine
(Also known as "early salting.") This is my favorite way to season a chicken — salt it the night before and let it cure in the refrigerator. At first, the salt pulls juices out of the meat. Then the brining effect takes

hold, and osmosis pulls the salt and juices back into the bird. That's right — we're brining the chicken in its own juices, intensifying the chicken flavor.

The downside to a dry brine is time. If the salt doesn't have at least an hour to work, osmosis doesn't start, and all the salt does is draw juices out of the bird. We get some of the advantages of dry brining after four hours. Eight hours is my shortest dry brining time, and I get the best results when I dry brine overnight in the fridge. If I'm cooking in less than eight hours, I move on to wet or injection brining.

The other secret to dry brining is the time spent in the refrigerator. A refrigerator is a very dry environment, and refrigerating the chicken dries out the skin. Water in the skin slows down browning, so drying the skin is a good thing, resulting in crisp, crackling, browned chicken.

You can dry brine as much as three days ahead of time. Cover the chicken with plastic wrap until 24 hours before cooking, so the chicken doesn't get too dehydrated.

Wet brine
Dry brines aren't really brines; a brine is defined as a salt and water combination. Wet brines are actual brines, where we soak a chicken in salty water. Wet brines plump up the chicken — as the water and salt are absorbed, the meat gets juicier — which is why commercial chicken processors often pre-brine chicken.

There are two downsides to wet brining. One is the water absorbed by the chicken. Wet brined chicken is juicier, but it is also a little watered down. Tastes differ; if you are a juicy white meat fan, you may prefer wet brining; I like the deeper chicken taste from dry brining.

The second downside to wet brining: it also brines the chicken skin. As I mentioned before, extra water in the skin makes it harder to brown and crisp up, because the extra water needs to evaporate before the skin will start browning.

I usually add sugar to my wet brines to counteract the wet skin. The sugar in the brine caramelizes on the skin of the bird, helping it brown quicker, even with the extra water.

One last downside to wet brining — dealing with all that salted water. We have to find a container large enough to submerge the chicken, and make room for it in the refrigerator. Then, when we're done, we have to pour the brine down the drain without splashing raw chicken juices and water all over the kitchen. (Not that I've ever done that...oh, no, not me.)

So, after all that — why wet brine?

First, the extra water has an upside — it is harder to overcook the chicken breast. Wet brined white meat can go as high as 165°F to 170°F before it dries out, so a wet brine is the way to go if you want some wiggle room when you're cooking.

Second, a wet brine works much faster than a dry brine; with a wet brine, the chicken is ready in 1 to 4 hours. My rule of thumb: if I buy a chicken the day before cooking, I use a dry brine; if I buy the chicken the day I'm cooking it, I use a wet brine.

Injection brine
Here's a new trick I learned from Modernist Cuisine, Nathan Myhrvold and Maxime Bilet's encyclopedia of food science.

Instead of soaking the chicken in a brine, inject the brine deep into the meat with a food safe syringe. Injection brining solves a lot of the problems with wet brines. The mess is contained; there's a much smaller amount of brine to deal with, and no big pot of chicken water to throw away afterward. The brine is injected where we need it, in the meat, so the chicken skin doesn't get brined. This makes the skin easy to crisp up on the grill. And, injection brining is fast. We don't have to wait for osmosis to absorb the brine deep into the meat; it's already there. The result is brined chicken, ready to go in an hour. (Though you can let it brine longer if you need to.)

You need a marinade injector for injection brine. Look for these jumbo syringes in the grilling supply section of your local hardware store, especially around Thanksgiving.

(Why Thanksgiving? Because injected deep fried turkey is a thing nowadays. Unfortunately, most of the injection marinades used for deep fried turkey have butter as the main ingredient. This doesn't brine the turkey; it just adds streaks of fat to the meat. Injection *brining* works great with turkey; double my injection brine recipes, and the white meat turkey lovers will thank you. Phew. I'm sorry I got sidetracked from chicken, but I had to get that off of my chest.)

Enhanced and Kosher Chicken
Watch out for "enhanced" chicken, "chicken in a 10% solution," or words to that effect on the packaging. Enhanced chicken is brined at the processing plant. Chicken processors pre-brine their birds because they don't trust us to cook chicken properly. If you're reading this, you don't need enhanced chicken.

I buy minimally processed natural chicken and brine it myself. (Why pay chicken prices for 10% water?) That said, when I accidentally re-brine an enhanced bird, it works fine — since it's already brined, not much of the extra brine gets absorbed.

Kosher birds are dry brined for an hour as part of the koshering process. They're a good choice if you want a subtle dry brining effect on a bird straight from the store. I use them every now and then when I'm in a hurry, but most of the time I want to do my own brining.

Marinades
Marinating is soaking in a flavorful liquid. Marinades do a good job of seasoning the outside of the bird, but they don't penetrate like a

brine. Traditional marinades don't have enough salt to get osmosis going, and flavor molecules are too big to penetrate into meat. But… why marinate when you can brinerate and get the best of both worlds?

Brinerades

I build my marinades with a lot of salt in them, often using soy sauce as a major ingredient. Brinerades season the outside of the bird like a marinade, while the salt penetrates deep into the meat like a brine.

Injection marinades

You can inject marinades deep into the chicken, but I'm not a fan. Injected marinades get the flavors deep into the meat, but like regular marinades, they don't penetrate beyond the needle tracks. I get streaks of marinade surrounded by large patches of unflavored meat. In general, I save my injection syringe for brining.

Dry rubs

Dry rubs are a powerful flavoring technique, a blend of spices and herbs sprinkled directly onto the chicken. The key to dry rubs is coverage — I want to spices all over the bird, inside and out. I start sprinkling into the cavity, concentrating on the inside of the thighs and the breasts. Then I dust the outside of the chicken, coating the whole bird in rub. Finally, I lift the skin and rub some spices directly onto the breast meat. Starting from the neck end of the bird, I gently work a finger between the skin and the breast meat. Then I spread a big pinch of spices under the skin, directly onto the breast meat.

Note that "rub" is not a good explanation of how I season the chicken. Applying a rub involves sprinkling and patting to make it stick, not a deep tissue massage. I try not to rub it too much, or the spices all end up on my hands instead of the chicken.

And, If you have the time, use the rub as a dry brine. Rub the chicken the early, and let it rest in the refrigerator overnight.

Seasoning pastes

Pastes are a cross between a dry rub and a marinade. I think of them as wet rubs — adding oil to a rub to turn it into a paste. (Think spreadable, not pourable.) I apply pastes like I do rubs — inside the chicken and out, then working some under the skin, directly on the breast meat.

Glazes and sauces

I think of glazes and sauces as another layer of flavor to the chicken; I use one of the seasoning methods above, then apply a glaze as a finishing touch. Most glazes have sugar in them, which will burn in the heat of the grill. To avoid carbonized glazes, I apply them to the chicken during the last fifteen minutes of cooking — long enough to tighten up into a glossy coat. Also, I like to apply the glaze in layers, brushing more on every five minutes to build up a thick coat.

Is It Done? (The Science of Cooking Chicken)

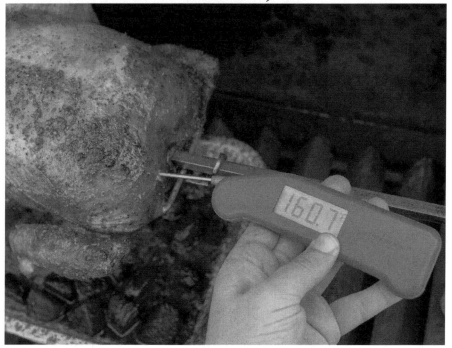

Cooking a whole chicken is a problem. A chef explained it like this: "You wouldn't put a whole cow in the oven and expect it to come out cooked properly, would you? So why would it work with a chicken?" (Unfortunately, I can't remember the chef, but his explanation stuck with me, because it makes so much sense.) Why is it so hard? Because we're dealing with different types of meat. Lean, tender white meat is best cooked to 150°F, while fatty, tougher dark meat is best cooked to 170°F or higher.

I was taught to cook chicken to 165°F. Why? Because that's the USDA recommended temperature for home cooks, based on their time and temperature charts for destroying salmonella.

For salmonella to be "killed," the USDA wants a 7 log reduction in the amount of salmonella in the meat. A "log reduction" is the logarithmic scale used to measure a reduction in live bacteria. Each log reduction means the bacteria are reduced by a factor of 10. In other words, 1 log reduction means killing 90% of the remaining bacteria; 2 log reduction kills 99%, 3 log reduction kills 99.9%, and so on. A 7 log reduction kills 99.99999% of the salmonella bacteria. (I hope this doesn't make you squeamish, but even at 7 log, 0.00001% of the salmonella bacteria are left. So, there is a chance that a tiny amount of salmonella survived…but it is such a small amount that it won't be dangerous.)

I learned that 165°F is the magic number because it is the high end of the USDA's a time/temperature curve for poultry. The USDA wants to be absolutely sure salmonella is dead, and at 165°F, salmonella is killed instantly. What I found interesting is the time/temperature curve. There is a whole range of time and temperature combinations that kill salmonella. On the other end of the scale, chicken can be safe cooked to 136°F, but only if it is held at 136°F for more than 81 minutes.

So, what's the problem with 165°F? Juicy meat. At 120°F, the muscle fibers in meat start to tighten up, squeezing out liquid. This moisture loss speeds up above 140°F. For the best balance of juiciness and cooking, we would eat chicken breast cooked to 140°F — medium-well, no longer pink in the middle, but before it lost too much moisture. I've tasted 140°F chicken breast, cooked in a sous vide water bath for an hour, and it is amazingly tender and juicy.

So, cook chicken to 140°F, hold it there for <checks chart> 35 minutes, and we're done, right? No, not so fast.

Let's talk about the dark side. If a muscle is in constant use, it is dark meat. Because chicken spends most of its time standing or walking around, the legs are dark meat. Flightless chickens have white breast meat, because the breast muscles don't get much use. (Ducks and geese have dark meat in the breast as well as the legs, because flying works out their breast muscles.)

Dark meat has more connective tissue; the muscles need it to do their work. Most of that connective tissue is made out of collagen, which is tough and chewy if undercooked. Collagen starts to break down at 160°F and turn into juicy gelatin, adding moisture to the meat. To break down collagen, we want to cook dark meat to at least 170°F, and higher temperatures are better. (It's hard to overcook chicken legs.)

Why is dark meat actually dark in color? Dark meat muscles do a lot of work over a long period of time, and need oxygen to work. If you've ever "felt the burn" while exercising, it's because your muscles wanted more oxygen. Dark meat muscles have a lot of myoglobin, a dark colored protein in the muscle fiber that stores oxygen. This stored oxygen lets a dark meat muscle work without needing to constantly pull oxygen from the bloodstream.

To sum up — chicken breast wants to be cooked to a low temperature; chicken legs need to be cooked to a high a temperature. What we're trying to do when roasting a whole chicken is balance out these two competing needs. I recommend cooking chicken until the breast reaches 160°F and pulling the chicken off the grill immediately. What about the dark meat? Trussing the chicken pushes the knobs of the drumsticks out, away from the body and closer to the heat of the grill. This cooks the legs faster than the breast; by the time the breast reaches 160°F, the legs should reach 170°F.

If you really want to improve your breast meat, here's a trick. Take the chicken out of the refrigerator an hour before cooking. Fill a quart sized zip-top bag full of ice, and lay it on top of the chicken breast, making sure the ice does not touch the drumsticks. After an hour, the breast will be chilled, but the legs will have warmed up. This gives the legs a head start on the breast meat.

(Do I actually I ice my chicken breasts? No. It's more effort than I'm willing to make for chicken. But I use this trick every year with my Thanksgiving turkey. Turkey breast has less fat than chicken breast, and dries out even faster, so it needs the extra help. If you really want the ultimate in juicy white meat with tender, gelatinous dark meat, icing the breasts is the way to go.)

On top of the white meat vs. dark meat issue is chicken skin. We want to render the layer of fat under the skin, or it will taste flabby. (Fat starts to melt at 130°F). As the fat melts, the skin starts to brown and crisp up.

And that brings us to browning, an entirely different branch of food science. Louis-Camille Maillard, a French food scientist, figured out protein browning. In his honor, the scientific name for browning is "the Maillard reaction".

Browning happens when protein is exposed to high temperatures, starting around 310°F. Because water boils at 212°F, wet chicken will not brown — the skin is stuck well below browning temperatures until the water evaporates. Meat juices and fat, however, are full of protein and good for browning. This is rotisserie's big advantage — the chicken bastes in its own juices. Instead of juices dripping off, the rotisserie rolls them around the outside of the chicken, exposing them to the heat of the grill, and increasing the browning. (Charcoal browns better than gas, by the way — gas burns with a wet heat, which slows down the browning reaction. For more details, see the "Charcoal or Gas?" chapter.)

In summary: with a rotisserie we get tender white meat, juicy dark meat, and crispy skin, all in one trussed bird. Simple, right?

CHARCOAL OR GAS?

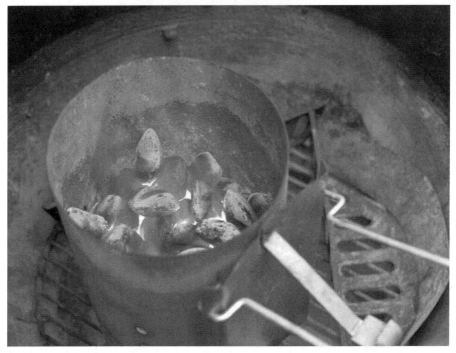

Time for the eternal grilling question: Charcoal or Gas? The answer is as personal as boxers or briefs.

Charcoal

Are you a charcoal person? Charcoal's advantages are:
- Better browning — burning charcoal releases lots of radiant heat, resulting in crackling chicken skin
- Charcoal burn down — starts out hot and slowly cools, gently finishing the chicken
- Inexpensive grill — a cheap charcoal grill outperforms all but the most expensive gas grills
- Better smoking — wood smoke is trapped in a charcoal grill, resulting in more smoke flavor in the chicken
- Purist factor — I'm a Real Man, I cook meat over hunks of burning wood. Charcoal is primal.

But, charcoal has some disadvantages:
- Less convenient — charcoal takes longer to light, and if I wait too long, it burns down and I lose the heat
- Messy — Have to deal with ash, soot, and bags of charcoal
- More expensive fuel — charcoal costs more than gas, on a per use basis

Gas
Or are you a gas person? Gas also has advantages:
- Convenient — the grill is ready in fifteen minutes, and will hold the temperature as long as we want
- Less expensive fuel — gas costs less than charcoal
- Weather resistant — gas grills are better insulated, and hold heat better in bad weather
- Status symbol - A huge, gleaming, stainless steel grill on the deck looks more impressive than a humble charcoal kettle.

Of course, gas has disadvantages:
- Not as hot as charcoal — burning gas does not produce as much radiant heat; food browns slower on a gas grill
- More expensive grill — gas grills, especially good gas grills, cost a lot more than charcoal grills
- Inferior smoking — wood smoke escapes through the vents in a gas grill

If I could only have one grill, it would be charcoal. Luckily, I don't have to choose. I use my charcoal kettle when I have the time, and my huge gas grill when I'm in a hurry…or the weather is conspiring against me.

I live in Northeastern Ohio. The weather is always conspiring against me.

Simulating charcoal burn down on a gas grill
One of the advantages of a gas grill can also be a disadvantage.

Charcoal starts with high heat, browning the chicken. Over time, the fire consumes the charcoal, and the temperature drops. The chicken cooks gently in the lower heat, slowly arriving at its final temperature.

A gas grill is set it and forget it — set the grill to high, and it stays there forever. (Or as long as we have gas in the tank. Not that I ever ran out of gas in the middle of a cook. Oh no, not me.) Leaving the grill set to high means the chicken zooms straight to the final temperature. It is easy to overcook a chicken on a gas grill if you get distracted at the end.

Here's how to simulate charcoal burn down on a gas grill. Start with the grill as hot as you can get it, preheating the grill for fifteen minutes with all the burners turned to high. Set up the grill for indirect high heat and start cooking the chicken. Check the bird after 30 minutes. If the chicken skin is browning well, or starting to get a little black in spots, turn the heat down to medium low, about 300°F. Finish the chicken at this lower heat. (On grills with an infrared burner, turn the IR burner off; on regular grills, turn down the outer burners to adjust the temperature.)

When do I use this trick? When the recipe has a rub or marinade, especially one with sugar or soy sauce. They burn if exposed to high heat for the entire cooking time, so I give the chicken 30 minutes to brown, then turn down the heat.

Does burn down affect cooking times? Yes…a little. But, not as much as you'd think — probably an extra five to ten minutes. Give yourself a little extra time, and please, use an instant read thermometer to check for doneness. (Please!)

Infrared Burners
Why are we seeing infrared burners on gas grills? Because charcoal browns better than gas.

To explain more, I need to go even farther into the science of heat and cooking protein.

There are three types of heat in cooking: radiation, convection, and conduction.

Radiation is emitted by burning fuel — in our case, either charcoal or gas. Waves of infrared radiation transmit heat directly to the food. Charcoal's advantage is radiation — burning charcoal produces a lot more infrared radiation than burning gas.

Convection is cooking with heated air. Burning fuel (gas or charcoal) heats the air in the grill, and the air heats the food. This is how most of the heat transfer occurs in both gas and charcoal grills — the heated air cooks the food. (And, this is why I ask you to keep the lid closed as while rotisserie grilling. Every time the lid opens, hot air escapes, slowing down the cooking.)

Conduction is cooking by direct transfer of heat between two surfaces. For conduction, you need a heated surface — a fry pan, a preheated grill grate — and the food goes directly onto the surface. Conduction doesn't play much of a role in rotisserie cooking; the spit doesn't heat up enough during its short time on the grill to conduct heat.

So, because charcoal emits a lot more radiated heat, a cheap charcoal grill browns better than an expensive gas grill. Gas grill manufacturers know this, and that's why they invented infrared burners. An infrared burner super-heats a ceramic plate, and the plate radiates heat, resulting in more infrared radiation than we get from burning the gas on its own.

Infrared rotisserie burners are a (relatively) new addition to high end grills — I started seeing them about ten years ago. IR burners help gas grills close the gap with charcoal. My gas grill has one, and I love it.

Most infrared rotisserie burners are not powerful enough to cook the chicken on their own. I use my infrared burner in combination with the traditional burners in my grill; the infrared burner gives me browning and some heat; the regular burners add enough heat to cook the chicken through with convection. Read your grill's manual, try your grill out, and see how much heat you can get with only the rotisserie burner. If your rotisserie burner can heat your entire grill, great! If not, turn on some of the regular burners until you get to at least 450°F for high heat, or 350°F for medium heat.

Equipment

It takes more than just a grill, a spit, and a motor to make rotisserie chicken. Here are the cooking tools and gadgets I use, from most important (something to protect your hands, butcher's twine) to least important (a marinade injector is nice to have, but far from essential.)

Heatproof Gloves
A hot rotisserie spit is a three foot long branding iron, so protecting your hands is an absolute necessity. I've used thick leather welding gloves for years. They are easy to slip on and off, come up to my forearms to protect my wrists, and they are cheap to buy at the hardware store. A lot of "grilling gloves" are essentially welding

gloves, where the only differences are the label and the price.

A new type of grilling glove has come out recently, based on technology used in fire fighting. The gloves are knitted out of Nomex, a heat resistant fiber. These gloves protect my hands like welding gloves, but have a much tighter fit. The tight fit allows me a lot more dexterity with my fingers — I can do finer work with the Nomex gloves on — but the tight fit makes it harder to slip the gloves off if I need a bare hand.

Which kind of glove should you get? I've been using them both, and I keep going back and forth about which I prefer. Both types of glove do a good job of protecting me from the heat of the spit. Try them on at the store, and get the glove that feels better on your hands.

Butcher's Twine
Trussing is critical for rotisserie chicken; we can't have the chicken flopping around on the spit. I buy cones of heavy duty cotton butcher's twine (sometimes called kitchen twine). Make sure to get plain twine, made of nothing but cotton. Watch out for waxed twine, which will leave your chicken tasting like candles. Stay away from candy-cane striped baker's twine. It may look pretty, but it has nylon in it, and melted nylon is not a good chicken seasoning.

Linen twine is even better than cotton, because linen burns at a higher temperature than cotton, but linen twine it is also more expensive. I go with less expensive cotton twine. The only time I've seen cotton twine burn in the rotisserie was when I forgot to trim a long tail of excess twine. It was hanging far away from the chicken, exposed to the heat without chicken juices to protect it. And, even then, the cotton twine was more singed than burned.

Drip Pans
Drip pans are another essential piece of equipment. Fat and juices drip off the chicken as it cooks on the rotisserie. The chicken is locked in place on the rotisserie, forcing everything to drip in the same exact

spot. Without a pan to catch the drippings, the grill will be a mess — a grease fire waiting to happen.

Disposable aluminum foil pans are the easy option. Put one on the grill under the chicken; when you're done cooking, toss the pan in the garbage, and the mess is gone. I buy stacks of half size steam table pans, roughly 10 by 12 inches, designed for serving in buffet steam tables. In my kettle grill I use Weber's elongated Extra Large drip pans, which are 6 by 14 inches and fit perfectly between the charcoal baskets. (Or, I fold and crimp the edges of a steam table pan to make it fit between my charcoal baskets.) If I'm really desperate, I'll fold a sheet of heavy duty aluminum foil into a pan shape and put it under the chicken; it's not pretty, but it catches the drips.

The problem with aluminum foil pans? Waste. I hate throwing them away after only one use. My solution is enameled steel roasting pans. Enameled steel is used for campfire cooking; standing up to the heat of a grill is no problem. When the cooking is done, scrub them out and they're ready for your next rotisserie session. The colorful speckled pans you see in my pictures are 11 by 13 inch "large roasting pans" from Crow Canyon; any enameled steel pan with roughly those dimensions will work.

Instant Read Thermometer
Using a thermometer is the best thing you can do for your chicken. We want the chicken breast cooked to 160°F, and not much more; the only way to know for sure is with a thermometer.

Analog instant read thermometers are cheap and available everywhere. They're not very precise, and they're not very fast, but you can usually get one for less than ten dollars. Look for a pocket thermometer with a thin probe — older meat thermometers with thick probes are not as accurate, and leave a huge hole in the chicken.

Digital thermometers are quick and precise. That said, "instant read" means about 10 seconds to register the temperature in cheaper digital thermometers. The thermometer I use every day is the Thermapen. It is extremely fast and accurate due to the thermocouple in its tip (most thermometers use a less expensive thermistor to measure temperature). I paid for that speed, though; as of this writing, a Thermapen costs around $90, while cheap digital thermometers cost $20 or so.

Which thermometer should you get? I love my Thermapen. I take it with me when I'm traveling, because I don't know what I'd do without it. But any thermometer, even a cheap one, is better than guessing if the chicken is done.

Kitchen Tongs
Kitchen tongs are my hands when I'm cooking. My favorites are 12 inch spring loaded tongs. (Shorter tongs don't keep me far enough from the heat of the grill; longer tongs are unwieldy.) With rotisserie chicken, tongs are most useful when it is time to take the cooked bird off of the spit. I use tongs to loosen the knobs on my spit forks, pull the fork out of the chicken, and then push the cooked chicken off of the spit. (That way, I don't touch the bird with my messy grilling gloves.)

Kitchen Scissors
Look for a heavy duty pair of kitchen scissors (also known as kitchen shears) that feel good in your hands. I prefer all purpose kitchen scissors with loop handles and short, straight blades. Kitchen scissors cut through twine, and also make a good tool for carving the chicken if you aren't comfortable carving with a knife.

I don't like poultry shears with long curved blades, bone notches, and straight handles without loops. The curved blade with bone notches makes it less useful in the kitchen, and the straight handles are hard to hold on to when I'm cutting through a chicken. "Regular" kitchen scissors work better on chicken than these supposed "poultry" shears.

Chef's Knife and Paring Knife

These are the two knives every cook needs. A chef's knife is an all purpose kitchen tool, used in everything from carving a chicken to mincing herbs to dicing onions. A paring knife is for fine work — cutting twine and trimming fat and skin from chicken. These two knives do everything I need in the kitchen — 80% of the time I use a chef's knife, and 15% of the time I use a paring knife. (The remaining 5% is split between a boning knife, a long slicing knife, and a serrated bread knife. They're useful to have, but a good chef's knife can stand in for all of them.)

Carving Board with a juice groove
When the chicken is done cooking, it needs a place to rest, and then to be carved. Carving a chicken releases a surprising amount of juices, even after a fifteen minute rest, so a carving board with a deep juice groove is a necessity. I like a 12 by 18 carving board, big enough to carve two chickens at once.

Marinade Injector
If you want to try injection brining, you need a giant syringe. Look for a food grade marinade injector with at least a two ounce capacity. If you're having trouble finding one, look near the turkey frying kits for a big syringe with the word "Cajun" on it — injection marinades are popular with Cajun deep fried turkey.

FAQ

I get a lot of questions at my blog, Dad Cooks Dinner, about rotisserie grilling. Here are the most common questions; if I don't answer your question in this section, drop me a line at my blog. I'll try to answer, and if the question is good enough I'll add it to the next edition of the book.

Smoking wood?
Q: Should I add smoking wood to my grill?
A: Of course! Smoking wood is always a good add-on to rotisserie chicken. Throw a chunk of wood on the coals, or a foil-wrapped pouch of wood chips on the burner, and your chicken is bathed in smoky flavor.

When it comes to smoking, a simple charcoal grill outperforms even the most expensive gas grill. Burning propane (or natural gas) creates combustion gases, and those gases need to escape, so gas grills are designed to have a lot of airflow. The smoke escapes from the grill before it has much of a chance to flavor the chicken. That said, don't give up on smoking wood if you have a gas grill. Some smoke flavor is better than none at all.

Chips or chunks?
Q: So, which should I use, wood chips or wood chunks?
A: It depends…

Charcoal grill: Use chunks of wood. They burn longer and generate more smoke. You can use wood chips in a charcoal grill, if that's all you have available, but chunks do a better job of smoking. I soak wood chunks for an hour before adding them to the grill…when I remember. Theoretically, I get more smoke from soaked wood, but it doesn't seem to make a big difference in the final flavor. If I forgot to soak the wood, I shrug and put the wood chunks on the coals anyhow.

Gas grill: Use soaked wood chips. Soak the chips for an hour and then drain them. Wrap the drained chips in an envelope of heavy duty aluminum foil and poke some holes in the foil to let the smoke escape. Put the envelope of chips on a burner cover directly over a lit burner. (If your gas grill has a built in smoker box, use it instead of the foil envelope. My grill has a smoking box with a dedicated burner, to make sure the chips keep smoking.)

Smoking wood types and preferences
Hickory is the most common smoking wood. You will immediately recognize the taste of hickory, because it is how we smoke bacon. (Don't worry — it works great on chicken, too.) My favorite smoking wood is oak cut from decommissioned wine barrels. I'm not sure if the wine adds anything extra to the taste, but the smell reminds me of touring wine cellars, which is always a good thing.

You can use just about any hard wood, fruit wood, or nut wood for smoking. I've had good results with apple, cherry, and pecan wood. Stay away from pine, or any other soft wood — they release creosote when they burn, which can be toxic. I think the flavor of mesquite overwhelms chicken, but some people swear by it.

Lighting charcoal
Q: How do I light charcoal?
A: My favorite method is a chimney starter. I stuff the bottom with two crumpled pieces of newspaper, and fill the top of the chimney with charcoal. When I light the paper, the chimney acts as...well, as a chimney, pulling the heat up through the charcoal. The coals are ready in about twenty minutes. I also use my chimney as a charcoal measuring device — a full chimney holds 60 coals, which is the right amount of charcoal for high heat. Three quarters full (45 coals) is medium heat, and half full (30 coals) is low heat.

On windy days, I spray the newspaper with a little bit of cooking oil before crumpling it up and adding it to the chimney. Usually a grease fire is a cooking disaster, but in this case it is an advantage. The oil acts as an accelerant; once it catches fire, it won't blow out until all the oil is burned up.

You can also use an electric charcoal starter, a loop of wire with a handle and an extension cord. They're slower than charcoal chimneys, but if you have an outlet near your grill they can be convenient.

I avoid lighter fluid. Supposedly the lighter fluid burns away, leaving nothing but charcoal, but I can always smell it. I will only use lighter fluid if I'm desperate (Which usually means grilling at the park, in one of those boxy steel grills on a post next to the picnic tables.)

Please, whatever you do, stay away from "instant light" charcoal. The coals are soaked with lighter fluid; that's how they light without any help. No matter how long they burn, there is always more lighter fluid in the coals. In other words, you're smoking your chicken with lighter fluid. That's not good eats.

I recently bought a charcoal kettle grill with a gas igniter. I fill the charcoal baskets with coals, turn on the gas, press the button, and a gas flame lights the coals. After five minutes the coals are started; I turn off the gas and let the charcoal finish lighting itself. The gas igniter is fast and convenient, and may be replacing my chimney as my favorite way to light charcoal.

I can't get high heat!
Q: What if my gas grill doesn't get hot enough? It only gets to 380°F when I turn off the middle burner for indirect heat.
A: This is a common problem with gas grills. Once the grill is set up for indirect heat, the remaining burners don't have enough power to brown the bird. Here are a few tricks for cooking with lower heat.

1. Buy a big chicken. A larger bird takes longer to cook, giving the skin extra time to brown. (As we discussed in the "Is it Done?" chapter, the skin has to render out the fat and evaporate any water before it starts to brown, so more cooking time equals more browning.) If your grill can manage 350°F (medium heat), go with a five pound or larger bird. On medium heat, a five pound chicken will take about an hour a half to cook. That extra thirty minutes gives the skin time to brown at medium heat.
2. Make sure the skin is completely dry before starting the chicken. Pat the bird with paper towels before seasoning it. Even better, rest the chicken overnight in the refrigerator to dehydrate the skin. (See The Best Simple Rotisserie Chicken recipe for details on dry brining, where we salt the chicken then rest it overnight in the refrigerator.)
3. Put something on the skin that browns quickly. See the recipes with rubs, glazes, and marinades. Almost all of them contain an ingredient that speeds up browning, like spices, sugar, and soy sauce. You'll get a gorgeous, mahogany bird without high heat.
4. All of the above. Get a five pound roasting chicken, use a spice rub as a dry brine, rest it overnight in the refrigerator, and glaze it at the end of cooking. Not only will the bird be beautifully browned, it will have layers of flavor.

5. Time for a second grill. Buy a charcoal kettle with the matching rotisserie attachment. (What? I'm always looking for an excuse to buy another grill.)

Counterweight
Q: How do I use the rotisserie counterweight?
A: Some rotisserie sets come with a counterweight to balance out the meat and reduce the strain on the motor. I have one, and…I never use it.

I gave up on the counterweight when I got my gas grill — it came with the same motor as my kettle grill's rotisserie, but the spit does not have a counterweight. I worried about this until I cooked heavy turkeys and large rib roasts on the gas grill's rotisserie without any problems.

If you follow my "how to spit" instructions, the chicken is balanced on the spit, and the counterweight isn't really needed. But, if you do want to counterweight, here's how. Spit the chicken, then remove the rotisserie motor from the mounting bracket. Set the spit in the grooves on the rotisserie bracket and let go. Gravity will take over, and after some wobbling, the heaviest part of the bird will rotate to the bottom. Wait for the chicken to stop rocking, then attach the counterweight to the spit pointing straight up. That sets the counter counterweight (weight is up) opposite the bird (weight is down). Pull the spit out of the bracket, re-mount the rotisserie motor, and plug the spit into the motor. Your spit is counterweighted and the chicken is ready to cook.

What kind of chicken?
Q: Should I get a fancy chicken? What kind? Organic, Free Range, Pasture Raised, Air Chilled, Kosher…
A: Rotisserie grilling can do wonders for cheap, $0.69 a pound chicken from the grocery store. But, with simple recipes, quality matters — the better the bird, the better the results. There are all sorts of fancy (and expensive) chickens available. What is the difference between, say, a free range bird and an organic bird?

Here is a rundown of the different types of chicken you can find:

- Organic — regulated by the USDA — Certified Organic chicken must eat organic feed, never use antibiotics, and be free range (see below). "Regulated by the USDA" is a good thing — there are regular and random inspections, with consequences if the rules aren't followed.
- Free Range — Another USDA regulated term. Free range chickens must have access to the outdoors. Now, "outdoors" can be anything from a pasture to a fenced in concrete pad, so this term doesn't mean as much as it could…but at least the bird might see daylight.
- Pasture Raised — The USDA does not regulate this term. The chicken actually lives on a pasture, and feeds by foraging in the grass. (Free range and organic birds usually eat chicken feed.) Generally, farmers call their chickens "pasture raised" because they don't think free range standards go far enough, and they want to explain why their chickens are better than free range. If pasture raised chicken interests you, get to know your farmer, so you know their definition of "pasture raised" matches yours.
- Air Chilled — Chicken processing usually involves chilling the chicken in water. Air chilled chicken uses refrigeration instead. Refrigeration is more expensive, but results in a better tasting bird, because the bird doesn't absorb extra water.
- Kosher — The bird is processed to meet Jewish religious restrictions, such as humane slaughter and the health of the animal. Kosher processing includes salting the bird to draw out the blood, so the birds are essentially brined at the processing plant. If I'm in a hurry, and don't have time to brine, I can buy a kosher bird and put it straight on the grill.
- Halal — The bird is processed to meet Muslim religious restrictions, such as humane slaughter and the health of the animal. Kosher and Halal are very similar rules; Kosher meat is acceptable to Muslims if Halal meat is not available. (My

apologies to Jewish and Muslim readers if I got the details wrong. As you can tell, I'm a cook, not a religious scholar.)
- Hormone Free — This is entirely marketing. The USDA outlawed hormones in poultry feed in the 1950s, so all chicken sold in the US is hormone free. Why do poultry processors put it on their packaging? I have two guesses. One, it sounds good. (Hormone free is a good thing, right?) Two, it heads off questions from consumers who don't know that hormones are banned.

What size chicken?
Q: What does broiler/fryer mean, anyhow?
A: Here are the USDA classifications for different chicken sizes:

- Rock Cornish hen, Cornish game hen — 5 weeks old or younger, ready to cook weight of 2 pounds or less.
- Broiler, fryer, broiler/fryer — 10 weeks or younger, ready to cook weight greater than two pounds, less than five pounds. **This is my usual chicken size for rotisserie grilling.**
- Roaster, roasting chicken — 8 to 12 weeks old, with a ready to cook weight of 5 pounds or more.
- Capon — neutered male chicken, younger than 4 months (usually 6 to 8 pounds).

I was surprised to find out that cornish game hens are actually young chickens — they're not a separate breed. And, the less said about capons, the better. (Hey, I'm a guy. I get squeamish just thinking about it.) But I don't let that stop me from eating them - they are great, especially if you have to serve a larger crowd.

How many chickens fit on a spit?
Q: Can I cook two chickens at the same time?
A: If they fit on the spit, absolutely! The more the merrier. Don't worry — it doesn't change the cooking time.

Cooking time is determined by the thickest part of the bird, and how long it takes the heat to penetrate into the middle of the meat. For a chicken, the thickest parts are the breasts and the joint that joins the thigh and the drumstick. Adding another bird to the spit doesn't change the thickness, so cooking time is the same no matter how many birds you squeeze on the spit.

I rarely cook one bird at a time. If I'm taking the time to set up the rotisserie, the extra work to truss and spit a second chicken is minor. (And I love leftover chicken — see the leftovers chapter for what to do with the extra bird.)

Q: I only have one pair of spit forks. Can I still cook two chickens?
A: If you have two sets of spit forks, adding a second bird is easy — secure the second bird with the second set of forks. If you only have one set of forks, push the birds together so they hold each other tight on the spit. To do this, use one fork to secure the tail end of one chicken. Then put the next chicken on the spit so they meet nose to tail. Push hard with the second fork, forcing the chickens together, before tightening the fork onto the spit.

RECIPES

THE BASICS

We'll start with the basic rotisserie chicken recipes everyone should have in their toolbox. Here are five simple, straightforward birds, with enough finesse to make simple mean "inspiring", not "plain".

First is my favorite recipe of all time: dry brined rotisserie chicken. Not just my favorite rotisserie chicken — my favorite recipe OF ALL TIME. If you make only one recipe in this book, make it the dry brined rotisserie chicken. I'll forgive you if you get stuck and make it over and over. This is the only recipe I duplicated from my Rotisserie Grilling cookbook. I couldn't leave my favorite chicken recipe out of my rotisserie chicken cookbook.

Others recipes in the running for my all time favorite: grilled porterhouse steak, shredded pork tacos, Texas red chili, and prime rib. But this chicken wins out over all of them.

But, even the best chicken ever can get boring. When you get tired of basic rotisserie chicken, move on to the rest of the chapter: an herb paste, garlic butter baste, brown sugar brine, and a pantry spice rub. These are my favorite seasoning techniques, simple and full of flavor, and they show off the versatility rotisserie chicken.

The Best Chicken Ever (Simple Dry Brined Chicken)

I'm starting with my favorite recipe of all time, a simple dry brined rotisserie chicken. Judy Rodgers taught me about the joy of simple, well prepared food, and about dry brining, in her wonderful Zuni Cafe Cookbook. Judy's chicken inspired this recipe; nothing fancy, just a properly seasoned chicken, with wood smoke and a rotisserie.

This recipe is all about the technique and the quality of the ingredients. A good bird is critical — buy the best one you can afford. Salting the night before lets the dry brine season the chicken all the way through. Wood smoke adds an extra layer of flavor. And, of course, the rotisserie cooks it perfectly, with crisp skin and tender meat.

Here it is: chicken lover's nirvana.

Ingredients

- 1 (4 pound) chicken
- 1 tablespoon kosher salt
- 1 teaspoon freshly ground black pepper
- Smoking wood: A fist sized chunk for a charcoal grill or 1 cup of wood chips for a gas grill

1. Dry brine the chicken

Season the chicken with the salt and pepper, inside and out. Gently work your fingers between the skin and the breast, then rub some of the salt and pepper directly onto the breast meat. Refrigerate overnight, or up to 48 hours ahead of time.

2. Truss and spit the chicken

One hour before cooking, remove the chicken from the refrigerator. Fold the wingtips underneath the wings, then truss the chicken. Skewer the chicken on the rotisserie spit, securing it with the spit forks. Let the chicken rest at room temperature while the grill pre-heats. Submerge the smoking wood in water and let it soak until the grill is ready.

3. Set the grill for indirect high heat

Set up the grill for indirect high heat with the drip pan in the middle of the grill.

4. Rotisserie the chicken

Put the spit on the grill, start the motor spinning, and center the drip pan under the chicken. Add the smoking wood to the fire, close the lid, and cook until the chicken reaches 160°F in the thickest part of the breast, about 1 hour.

5. Serve

Remove the chicken from the rotisserie spit and then remove the trussing twine. Be careful — the spit and forks are blazing hot. Let the chicken rest for 15 minutes, then carve and serve.

THYME AND GARLIC PASTE CHICKEN

I'm not a gardener. I'm too easily distracted. (Watering? What's that?) I start gardens with the best of intentions, but eventually I stop paying attention, and weeds overrun it.

Then there are the plants that survive in spite of my indifference. Thyme will not be stopped. I planted herbs in the strip of dirt between my front walk and my garage, and the thyme bush is thriving, taking over everything.

So, every summer I have a lot of thyme on my hands. I use thyme in everything, from flavoring stews to garnishing vegetables, but my favorite is a thyme and garlic herb paste. This paste goes well with pork and beef, and it is fantastic on rotisserie chicken.

Ingredients
- 1 (4 pound) chicken

Herb paste

- 1 tablespoon kosher salt
- 2 teaspoons minced fresh thyme
- 2 cloves garlic, minced
- 1/2 teaspoon freshly ground black pepper
- 1 tablespoon olive oil

1. Rub the chicken
Mix the herb paste ingredients in a small bowl. Rub the chicken with the paste, inside and out. Gently work your fingers between the skin and the breast, then rub some of the paste directly onto the breast meat. Fold the wingtips under the wings and truss the chicken. Skewer the chicken on the rotisserie spit, securing it with the spit forks. Let the chicken rest at room temperature until the grill is ready.

2. Set the grill for indirect high heat
Set up the grill for indirect high heat with the drip pan in the middle of the grill.

3. Rotisserie the chicken
Put the spit on the grill, start the motor spinning, and center the drip pan under the chicken. Close the lid and cook until the chicken reaches 160°F in the thickest part of the breast, about 1 hour.

4. Serve
Remove the chicken from the rotisserie spit and then remove the trussing twine. Be careful — the spit and forks are blazing hot. Let the chicken rest for 15 minutes, then carve and serve.

GARLIC BUTTER BASTE CHICKEN

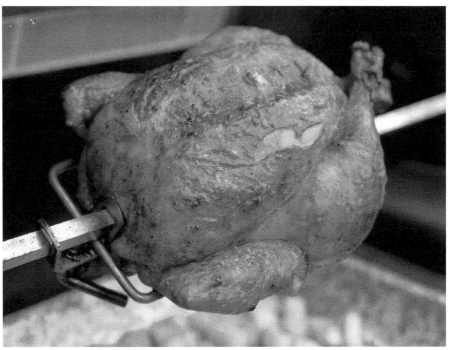

Julia Child said:

"I always give my bird a generous butter massage before I put it in the oven. Why? Because I think the chicken likes it. And, more important, I like to give it."

Would I argue with Julia Child? No, of course not. But…I am worried about the butter burning in the heat of the grill. Instead of a generous butter massage, I use a gentle butter bath. I baste the chicken with melted butter and garlic during the last 15 minutes of cooking. I hope Julia approves.

Ingredients
- 1 (4 pound) chicken
- 1 tablespoon kosher salt
- 1 teaspoon freshly ground black pepper

Garlic Butter Baste
- 4 tablespoons (half a stick) butter
- 2 cloves garlic, crushed

1. Prep the chicken
Season the chicken with the salt and pepper, inside and out. Gently work your fingers between the skin and the breast, then rub some of the salt and pepper directly onto the breast meat. Fold the wingtips underneath the wings, then truss the chicken. Skewer the chicken on the rotisserie spit, securing it with the spit forks. Let the chicken rest at room temperature while the grill pre-heats.

2. Set the grill for indirect high heat
Set up the grill for indirect high heat with the drip pan in the middle of the grill.

3. Melt the garlic butter baste
Put the butter and garlic in a small saucepan over medium heat. Simmer until the butter melts and the garlic starts sizzling, about three minutes. Remove from the heat and set aside for later.

4. Rotisserie the chicken
Put the spit on the grill, start the motor spinning, and center the drip pan under the chicken. Close the lid and cook until the chicken reaches 160°F in the thickest part of the breast, about 1 hour. During the last 15 minutes of cooking, brush the chicken with the garlic butter baste every five minutes.

5. Serve
Remove the chicken from the rotisserie spit and then remove the trussing twine. Be careful — the spit and forks are blazing hot. Brush with one last coat of garlic butter, then let the chicken rest for 15 minutes. Carve and serve.

BROWN SUGAR BRINE CHICKEN

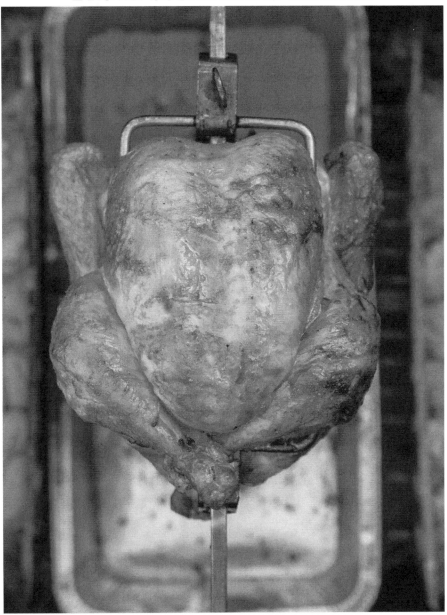

I know I told you I prefer dry brined chicken to wet brined. But a wet brined chicken is much better than an un-brined bird…and wet brining works faster. If I want to cook a chicken the day I bought it, I stir up a batch of this wet brine to season it quickly.

(Quick is a relative term here — a four hour brine is quick when compared to an overnight dry brine, right?)

The salt is what penetrates in a brine; sugar and peppercorn flavor molecules are too large to penetrate into the meat. That's OK. They season the outside of the bird, adding a hint of sweet and spice to the browned, crispy skin while the salt deep seasons the chicken.

Ingredients
- 1 (4 pound) chicken

Brine
- 3 quarts cold water
- 1/3 cup table salt (or 1/2 cup kosher salt)
- 1/4 cup brown sugar
- 1 tablespoon peppercorns, crushed or coarsely ground using the largest setting on your pepper mill

1. Brine the chicken
Stir the brine ingredients in large container until the salt and sugar dissolve. Submerge the chicken in the brine. Move the container to the refrigerator and brine the chicken for four to eight hours.

2. Truss and spit the chicken
Remove the chicken from the brine and pat dry with paper towels. Fold the wingtips underneath the wings, then truss the chicken. Skewer the chicken on the rotisserie spit, securing it with the spit forks. Let the chicken rest at room temperature until the grill is ready.

3. Set the grill for indirect high heat
Set up the grill for indirect high heat with the drip pan in the middle of the grill.

4. Rotisserie the chicken

Put the spit on the grill, start the motor spinning, and center the drip pan under the chicken. Close the lid and cook until the chicken reaches 160°F in the thickest part of the breast, about 1 hour.

5. Serve

Remove the chicken from the rotisserie spit and then remove the trussing twine. Be careful — the spit and forks are blazing hot. Let the chicken rest for 15 minutes, then carve and serve.

SPICE RUB CHICKEN

Spice rubs give chicken a quick layer of flavor — perfect if you're in a hurry. The main ingredient in this rub is paprika; it adds a sweet, mild flavor that the other spices build on. Next I add garlic, cumin, and coriander — a classic trio. Finally, a little black pepper and dry mustard add a hint of heat to the rub, just enough to give it a tingle at the end.

I have all these spices in my pantry, so this is a rub I will mix up on the spot if I need it. But, if I'm organized, I mix up a big batch; then I have a jar of rub ready for chicken (or pork) whenever I need it.

Ingredients
- 1 (4 pound) chicken

Spice Rub
- 1 tablespoon kosher salt

- 1 tablespoon sweet paprika
- 1 teaspoon garlic powder
- 1 teaspoon ground cumin
- 1 teaspoon ground coriander
- 1 teaspoon freshly ground black pepper
- 1/2 teaspoon dry mustard powder

1. Rub the chicken
Mix the spice rub ingredients in a small bowl. Sprinkle the chicken with the rub, inside and out, patting it onto the chicken to help it stick. Gently work your fingers between the skin and the breast, then work some of the rub directly onto the breast meat. Fold the wingtips under the wings and truss the chicken. Skewer the chicken on the rotisserie spit, securing it with the spit forks. Let the chicken rest at room temperature until the grill is ready.

2. Set the grill for indirect high heat
Set up the grill for indirect high heat with the drip pan in the middle of the grill.

3. Rotisserie the chicken
Put the spit on the grill, start the motor spinning, and center the drip pan under the chicken. Close the lid and cook until the chicken reaches 160°F in the thickest part of the breast, about 1 hour.

4. Serve
Remove the chicken from the rotisserie spit and then remove the trussing twine. Be careful — the spit and forks are blazing hot. Let the chicken rest for 15 minutes, then carve and serve.

BRINES, WET AND DRY

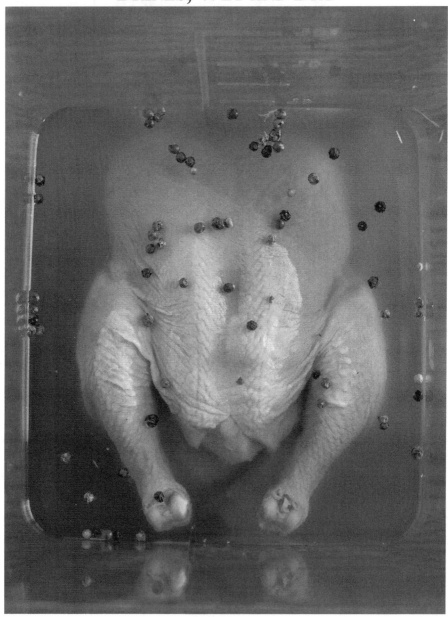

Brines are my favorite way to season chicken. With a brine, salt penetrates deep into the meat, seasoning the chicken all the way through.

The first brine I discovered is the traditional wet brine, where a soak in salted water seasons the chicken and adds extra moisture to white meat. And it was great!

Then I learned about dry brines, with all the seasoning of a wet brine but none of the extra moisture, so the chicken skin stays dry and crisps up. It was even better!

Recently I've started playing with injection brines. They add moisture like a wet brine, but only where I want it — deep inside the meat.

Which one is the best? That's a matter of personal taste. I use dry brines more often than the other two, but I like having all three styles available to me. With the recipes in this chapter, you can try out different brines and find your own favorite.

Here are my brining ratios, in case you want to build your own brine:

For a dry brine, I use 1/4 tablespoon of kosher salt per pound of chicken. So, a 3 pound bird needs 3/4 tablespoon of salt, a 4 pound bird needs 1 tablespoon of salt, a 5 pound bird needs 1 1/4 tablespoons of salt, and so on. If you're using table salt, cut the numbers in half — a four pound bird needs 1/2 a tablespoon of table salt, and so on. For fine sea salt, use 75% of the salt — a four pound bird needs 3/4 tablespoon of fine sea salt, and so forth. (Why do the amounts change? See the Seasoning chapter for details on salting by weight.)

For a wet brine, I use 1/4 cup of table salt per quart of water, and brine the chicken for 4 to 8 hours. Why do I switch to table salt? Because it's cheaper than kosher salt, and after dissolving, there is no difference between the two. If you have to use Kosher salt, double the amount of salt - 1/2 cup per quart of water. If you need to brine for a very long time — overnight, or up to 24 hours — cut the amount of salt in half, to 1/8 cup (2 tablespoons) of table salt per quart of water.

For an injection brine, I use the same ratio of salt to water as a wet brine - 1/4 cup of table salt to a quart of water. But, because I don't need to submerge the bird, I cut the total amount in half and use 2 tablespoons of table salt in 2 cups of water. Because the brine is already in the bird, the brining time can be as little as one hour; I'll go up to eight hours at the most.

Lemon and Fennel Dry Brine Chicken

Lemon and fennel are a classic Italian combination. Here, I use that flavor profile as the base of a dry brine.

Unfortunately, brining doesn't bring those flavors into the meat. Flavor molecules are too big to penetrate the meat through osmosis. But, that's OK — the salt in the dry brine will deep season the chicken. The lemon, fennel and peppercorns add a spicy crust on the outside of the bird. The result is layers of flavor, and a fantastic chicken.

I coarsely grind the fennel and peppercorns in a mortar and pestle, then stir in the salt and zest. If you don't have a mortar and pestle, improvise one with a coffee mug and a spice jar to grind the spices.

Ingredients
- 1 (4 pound) chicken

Lemon Fennel Dry Brine

- 1 tablespoon kosher salt (1 1/2 teaspoons table salt, 2 teaspoons fine sea salt)
- Zest of 1 lemon, minced
- 2 teaspoons fennel seed, coarsely ground
- 1 teaspoon black peppercorns, coarsely ground

1. Dry brine the chicken
Mix the dry brine ingredients until the lemon zest is evenly distributed. Season the chicken with the dry brine, inside and out. Gently work your fingers between the skin and the breast, then rub some of the spices directly onto the breast meat. Refrigerate overnight, or up to 48 hours ahead of time.

2. Truss and spit the chicken
One hour before cooking, remove the chicken from the refrigerator. Fold the wingtips underneath the wings, then truss the chicken. Skewer the chicken on the rotisserie spit, securing it with the spit forks. Let the chicken rest at room temperature while the grill preheats.

3. Set the grill for indirect high heat
Set up the grill for indirect high heat with the drip pan in the middle of the grill.

4. Rotisserie the chicken
Put the spit on the grill, start the motor spinning, and center the drip pan under the chicken. Close the lid and cook until the chicken reaches 160°F in the thickest part of the breast, about 1 hour.

5. Serve
Remove the chicken from the rotisserie spit and then remove the trussing twine. Be careful — the spit and forks are blazing hot. Let the chicken rest for 15 minutes, then carve and serve.

Coriander and Mixed Pepper Dry Brine Chicken

Coriander and pepper are a great combination; the French Canadians have been using Mignonette pepper, a blend of black peppercorns, white peppercorns, and coriander seed for years. For this recipe, I sub in a peppercorn blend for the black and white pepper, adding green and pink peppercorns to the mix.

When I'm grinding the spices in my mortar and pestle, I try not to grind them to a powder. Large pieces of coarsely ground pepper and coriander add bursts of flavor as you bite into them; it elevates this from a simple spice blend into something more.

Ingredients
- 1 (4 pound) chicken
- 1 tablespoon kosher salt

Coriander peppercorn blend
- 2 teaspoons peppercorn blend
- 1/2 teaspoon coriander seed

1. Dry brine the chicken
Coarsely grind the peppercorns and coriander in a spice grinder or mortar and pestle, then mix with the salt. Season the chicken with the blend, inside and out. Gently work your fingers between the skin and the breast, then rub some of the blend directly onto the breast meat. Refrigerate overnight, or up to 48 hours ahead of time.

2. Truss and spit the chicken
One hour before cooking, remove the chicken from the refrigerator. Fold the wingtips underneath the wings, then truss the chicken. Skewer the chicken on the rotisserie spit, securing it with the spit forks. Let the chicken rest at room temperature while the grill preheats. Submerge the smoking wood in water and let it soak until the grill is ready.

3. Set the grill for indirect high heat
Set up the grill for indirect high heat with the drip pan in the middle of the grill.

4. Rotisserie the chicken
Put the spit on the grill, start the motor spinning, and center the drip pan under the chicken. Close the lid and cook until the chicken reaches 160°F in the thickest part of the breast, about 1 hour.

5. Serve
Remove the chicken from the rotisserie spit and then remove the trussing twine. Be careful — the spit and forks are blazing hot. Let the chicken rest for 15 minutes, then carve and serve.

Apple Cider Wet Brine Chicken

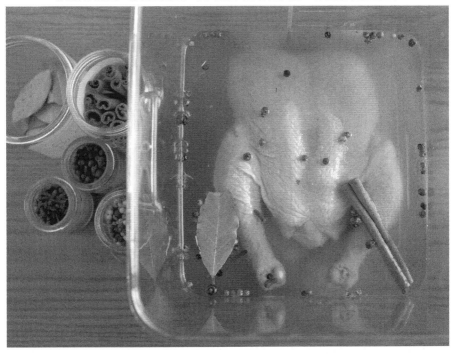

This brine is my salute to fall. It reminds me of a trip to the orchard, picking out a pumpkin, and walking through the trees, my feet crunching on the fallen leaves. And, when I'm done with my walk, a mug of hot apple cider by the fire.

It's that mulled cider that inspires this brine. A little sweet, a little spicy, it makes a delightful seasoning for chicken.

Ingredients
- 1 (4 pound) chicken

Apple Cider Brine
- 1 quart cold water
- 1 quart apple cider
- 1/2 cup table salt (or 1 cup kosher salt)
- 2 tablespoons brown sugar

- 2 bay leaves
- 1 stick cinnamon
- 5 whole allspice berries
- 3 whole cloves
- 1 tablespoon whole peppercorns

1. Brine the chicken
Combine the brine ingredients in large container and stir until the salt and brown sugar dissolve. Submerge the chicken in the brine. Move the container to the refrigerator and brine the chicken for four to eight hours.

2. Truss and spit the chicken
Remove the chicken from the brine and pat dry with paper towels, inside and out. Fold the wingtips underneath the wings, then truss the chicken. Skewer the chicken on the rotisserie spit, securing it with the spit forks. Let the chicken rest at room temperature until the grill is ready.

3. Set the grill for indirect high heat
Set up the grill for indirect high heat with the drip pan in the middle of the grill.

4. Rotisserie the chicken
Put the spit on the grill, start the motor spinning, and center the drip pan under the chicken. Close the lid and cook until the chicken reaches 160°F in the thickest part of the breast, about 1 hour.

5. Serve
Remove the chicken from the rotisserie spit and then remove the trussing twine. Be careful — the spit and forks are blazing hot. Let the chicken rest for 15 minutes, then carve and serve.

INJECTION BRINE CHICKEN

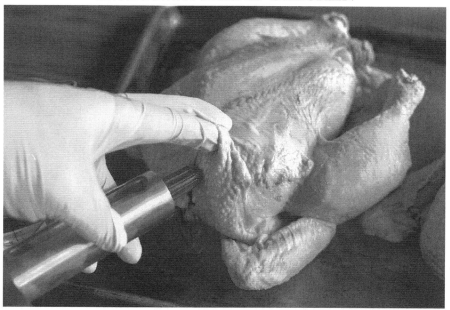

I picked up the Injection brining technique from Modernist Cuisine at Home, the massive, obsessive, science-based cookbook by Nathan Mhyrvold and Maxime Bilet. (Obsessive science-based cookbook? How could I resist?)

Injecting the brine deep into the meat, right where we want it, keeps the skin dry so it will crisp up. Cleanup is easy compared to the quarts of chicken-contaminated water left over by a traditional brine.

The downside to injection brining? Needles. I hate needles. As a kid, the nurses had to hold me down to give me vaccinations. I'm older and wiser now - I take my shots without complaint, and I'll set aside my fear of needles when it gives me a tasty chicken.

Equipment
- Marinade injector (a large syringe designed for injecting food)

Ingredients

- 1 (4 pound) chicken

Injection Brine
- 1 cup water
- 1 tablespoon kosher salt (1 1/2 teaspoons table salt)
- 1 teaspoon sugar

1. Inject the brine into the chicken
In a tall cup, stir the brine ingredients until the salt and sugar dissolve. Inject the brine into the meat of the bird, spacing the injections about an inch apart. Push the needle deep into the chicken and depress the plunger until the meat starts to swell. Then, slowly pull the needle out while pushing on the plunger, filling the entire needle hole with brine. Inject the breasts straight in from the front of the bird, through the neck cavity. Each side of the breast gets three long injections. Next, inject the thighs and the drumsticks, working through the cavity in the back of the bird as much as possible. (Injecting the drumstick may involve poking holes through the skin on the leg — that's OK, it's unavoidable.) There will be more brine than you need — I make extra rather than trying to suck up the last little bit into the syringe. Refrigerate the injected chicken for one to eight hours.

2. Truss and spit the chicken
Remove the chicken from the refrigerator. Fold the wingtips underneath the wings, then truss the chicken. Skewer the chicken on the rotisserie spit, securing it with the spit forks. Let the chicken rest at room temperature until the grill is ready.

3. Set the grill for indirect high heat
Set up the grill for indirect high heat with the drip pan in the middle of the grill.

4. Rotisserie the chicken
Put the spit on the grill, start the motor spinning, and center the drip

pan under the chicken. Close the lid and cook until the chicken reaches 160°F in the thickest part of the breast, about 1 hour.

5. Serve

Remove the chicken from the rotisserie spit and then remove the trussing twine. Be careful — the spit and forks are blazing hot. Let the chicken rest for 15 minutes, then carve and serve.

Soy Injection Brine Chicken

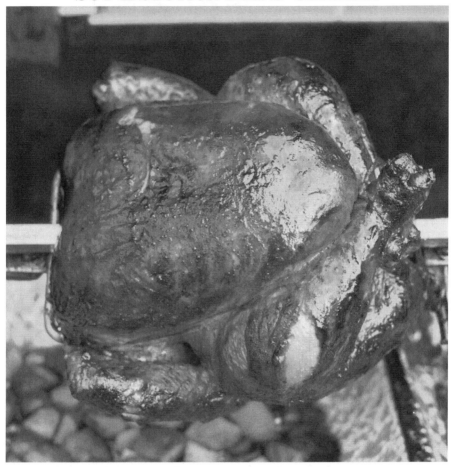

Soy sauce has the same water to salt ratio as a brine. This is why marinades based on soy sauce work so well — they're not just marinating, they're actually brining the bird.

I don't want to use the soy sauce as a marinade in this recipe; I'm injection brining with it. Normally, with an injection brine, I want to avoid getting the brine on the chicken skin to keep it dry. But, soy sauce has enough protein to help with browning. I baste the chicken with soy sauce during the last fifteen minutes of cooking to give the skin a gorgeous mahogany color.

Equipment
- Marinade injector (a large syringe designed for injecting food)

Ingredients
- 1 (4 pound) chicken

Injection Brine
- 1 cup soy sauce
- 2 tablespoons honey

Soy sauce baste
- 1 tablespoon soy sauce
- 1/2 teaspoon smoked Spanish paprika (or sweet paprika)

1. Inject the brine into the chicken

In a tall cup, whisk the brine ingredients until the honey dissolves. Inject the brine into the meat of the bird, spacing the injections about an inch apart. Push the needle deep into the chicken and depress the plunger until the meat starts to swell. Then, slowly pull the needle out while pushing on the plunger, filling the entire needle hole with brine. Inject the breasts straight in from the front of the bird, through the neck cavity. Each side of the breast gets three long injections. Next, inject the thighs and the drumsticks, working through the cavity in the back of the bird as much as possible. (Injecting the drumstick may involve poking holes through the skin on the leg — that's OK, it's unavoidable.) There will be more brine than you need — I make extra rather than trying to suck up the last little bit into the syringe. Refrigerate the injected chicken for one to eight hours.

2. Truss and spit the chicken

Remove the chicken from the refrigerator and pat dry with paper towels. Fold the wingtips underneath the wings, then truss the chicken. Skewer the chicken on the rotisserie spit, securing it with the spit forks. Let the chicken rest at room temperature until the grill is ready.

3. Set the grill for indirect high heat
Set up the grill for indirect high heat with the drip pan in the middle of the grill.

4. Rotisserie the chicken
Put the spit on the grill, start the motor spinning, and center the drip pan under the chicken. Close the lid and cook until the chicken reaches 160°F in the thickest part of the breast, about 1 hour. When there are fifteen minutes left to cook, brush the chicken with the soy sauce baste.

5. Serve
Remove the chicken from the rotisserie spit and then remove the trussing twine. Be careful — the spit and forks are blazing hot. Let the chicken rest for 15 minutes, then carve and serve.

Grocery Store Seasonings

Store bought seasoning blends are convenient — just sprinkle and go. I keep a couple different jars in my pantry for emergency seasoning situations. But…there's a catch.

Most of the time, we pay spice prices for blends that are mostly salt. Check the ingredient list; ingredients are listed in order, most used to least used. If the first ingredient is salt, there is more salt in the blend than anything else. (If the next ingredient is paprika, it is the next most used, and so on down the list.)

There is something to be said for the convenience of store bought spice blends; sometimes I'm willing to pay extra for that convenience. But, if there's a blend I use a lot, I'll reverse engineer it. I buy the individual spices, make a big batch, and store it in a jar in my pantry. That way I'm paying spice prices for spices, not salt. (See the spice rubs and barbecued birds chapters for some examples of homemade spice blends.)

And, there are times when I happily pay for store spice blends. One is when the blend is made entirely out of spices, with no salt added. Herbes de Provence is an example — it is entirely dried herbs. Some blends have obscure ingredients which are hard to find, or expensive if you buy them on their own. Za'atar seasoning is a good example — it is easier for me to find Za'atar blend than to find dried sumac, one of the key ingredients.

And, don't forget about dry brining. Any seasoning blend with salt can be used as a dry brine. Season the chicken and let it rest overnight in the refrigerator, and the salt will have time to season the bird all the way through.

SEASONED SALT CHICKEN

Lawrence Frank, owner of Lawry's The Prime Rib restaurant in Beverly Hills, created his seasoned salt in 1922. It was so popular that they started selling it to customers at the restaurant, and in 1938 they packaged it and started selling it in stores. Now you can find shakers of Lawry's Seasoned Salt in every grocery store in the country, where it supposedly outsells regular table salt!

Ingredients
- 1 (4 pound) chicken
- 1 tablespoon Seasoned Salt

1. Rub the chicken
Sprinkle the chicken with the seasoned salt, inside and out, patting it onto the chicken to help it stick. Gently work your fingers between the skin and the breast, then rub some of the seasoned salt directly onto the breast meat. Fold the wingtips under the wings and truss the

chicken. Skewer the chicken on the rotisserie spit, securing it with the spit forks. Let the chicken rest at room temperature until the grill is ready.

2. Set the grill for indirect high heat
Set up the grill for indirect high heat with the drip pan in the middle of the grill.

3. Rotisserie the chicken
Put the spit on the grill, start the motor spinning, and center the drip pan under the chicken. Close the lid and cook until the chicken reaches 160°F in the thickest part of the breast, about 1 hour.

4. Serve
Remove the chicken from the rotisserie spit and then remove the trussing twine. Be careful — the spit and forks are blazing hot. Let the chicken rest for 15 minutes, then carve and serve.

Montreal Steak Seasoning Chicken

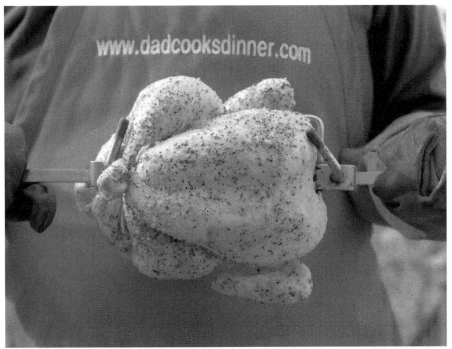

Montreal Steak Seasoning was originally a pickling spice blend, used on smoked meats in a Montreal deli. An intrepid employee started using the spices on grilled steaks; they became wildly popular. Soon, the idea spread to other delis and steak houses in Montreal, and they started making their own house blends. A culinary classic was born.

Now, you may ask: steak seasoning? On a chicken? Absolutely. I use the original steak seasoning on any and all meats. I think "Montreal Chicken" blends are spice company marketing — they want you to buy two bottles of spices instead of just one.

Ingredients
- 1 (4 pound) chicken
- 1 1/2 tablespoons Montreal Steak seasoning

1. Rub the chicken

Sprinkle the chicken with the Montreal Steak seasoning, inside and out, patting it onto the chicken to help it stick. Gently work your fingers between the skin and the breast, then rub some of the seasoning directly onto the breast meat. Fold the wingtips under the wings and truss the chicken. Skewer the chicken on the rotisserie spit, securing it with the spit forks. Let the chicken rest at room temperature until the grill is ready.

2. Set the grill for indirect high heat
Set up the grill for indirect high heat with the drip pan in the middle of the grill.

3. Rotisserie the chicken
Put the spit on the grill, start the motor spinning, and center the drip pan under the chicken. Close the lid and cook until the chicken reaches 160°F in the thickest part of the breast, about 1 hour.

4. Serve
Remove the chicken from the rotisserie spit and then remove the trussing twine. Be careful — the spit and forks are blazing hot. Let the chicken rest for 15 minutes, then carve and serve.

HERBES DE PROVENCE CHICKEN

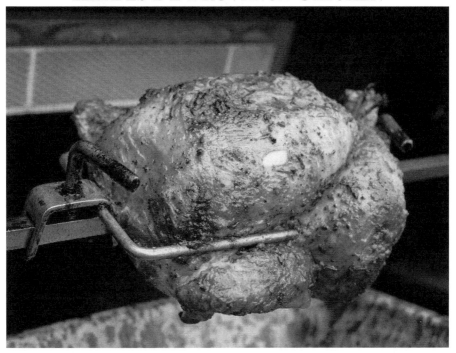

Years ago, I took a week of cooking classes in the French hill town of Roussillon, Provence. Someday I will return; until then, I have my jar of Herbes de Provence to take me back. It is built on a blend of savory, thyme, fennel, basil, and rosemary; but each Provencal cook usually adds their own secret ingredients to personalize the blend.

I serve this chicken on a hot summer day with a chilled bottle of French Rosè; I pretend I'm looking out over the hills of the Luberon. Someday I'll get back to Provence. Someday…

Ingredients
- 1 (4 pound) chicken
- 1 tablespoon kosher salt
- 1 tablespoon Herbes De Provence seasoning

1. Rub the chicken

Mix the salt and the Herbes de Provence in a small bowl. Sprinkle the chicken with the seasoning mix, inside and out, patting it onto the chicken to help it stick. Gently work your fingers between the skin and the breast, then rub some of the seasoning directly onto the breast meat. Fold the wingtips under the wings and truss the chicken. Skewer the chicken on the rotisserie spit, securing it with the spit forks. Let the chicken rest at room temperature until the grill is ready.

2. Set the grill for indirect high heat
Set up the grill for indirect high heat with the drip pan in the middle of the grill.

3. Rotisserie the chicken
Put the spit on the grill, start the motor spinning, and center the drip pan under the chicken. Close the lid and cook until the chicken reaches 160°F in the thickest part of the breast, about 1 hour.

4. Serve
Remove the chicken from the rotisserie spit and then remove the trussing twine. Be careful — the spit and forks are blazing hot. Let the chicken rest for 15 minutes, then carve and serve.

Adobo Seasoning Chicken

The Adobo seasoning you'll find in the Latin foods aisle at your grocery store is from Puerto Rico. This seasoned salt includes garlic, onion, oregano, and hot pepper. It should not to be confused with Puerto Rican wet adobos, Mexican adobo pastes, or any of the other variations on adobo in the Spanish speaking world. Adobo means "seasoning" or "marinade" in Spanish, and it takes on wildly different forms in different countries.

Ingredients
- 1 (4 pound) chicken
- 1 tablespoon Adobo seasoning

1. Rub the chicken
Sprinkle the chicken with the Adobo seasoning, inside and out, patting it onto the chicken to help it stick. Gently work your fingers between the skin and the breast, then rub some of the seasoning

directly onto the breast meat. Fold the wingtips under the wings and truss the chicken. Skewer the chicken on the rotisserie spit, securing it with the spit forks. Let the chicken rest at room temperature until the grill is ready.

2. Set the grill for indirect high heat
Set up the grill for indirect high heat with the drip pan in the middle of the grill.

3. Rotisserie the chicken
Put the spit on the grill, start the motor spinning, and center the drip pan under the chicken. Close the lid and cook until the chicken reaches 160°F in the thickest part of the breast, about 1 hour.

4. Serve
Remove the chicken from the rotisserie spit and then remove the trussing twine. Be careful — the spit and forks are blazing hot. Let the chicken rest for 15 minutes, then carve and serve.

ZATAR CHICKEN

Za'atar is a spice blend used across North Africa and the Middle East. Supposedly, every housewife has her own Za'atar blend that she mixes up to season her food. The ingredients in the blend change as you travel across the region, but it usually includes thyme, sumac, sesame seeds, and salt.

Za'atar has a bunch of different spellings — zaatar, zatar, za'tar, zahtar — the result of romanizing the word. (That is, figuring out how an Arabic word should be spelled in English.) This might be the trickiest spice blend to find in this book; it may require a trip to your local Middle Eastern market or specialty spice shop. That said, I see it occasionally at gourmet grocery and specialty spice shops.

Ingredients
- 1 (4 pound) chicken
- 1 1/2 tablespoons Za'atar seasoning

- 1/2 tablespoon kosher salt

1. Rub the chicken

Mix the salt and the Za'atar seasoning in a small bowl. Sprinkle the chicken with the seasoning mix, inside and out, patting it onto the chicken to help it stick. Gently work your fingers between the skin and the breast, then rub some of the seasoning directly onto the breast meat. Fold the wingtips under the wings and truss the chicken. Skewer the chicken on the rotisserie spit, securing it with the spit forks. Let the chicken rest at room temperature until the grill is ready.

2. Set the grill for indirect high heat

Set up the grill for indirect high heat with the drip pan in the middle of the grill.

3. Rotisserie the chicken

Put the spit on the grill, start the motor spinning, and center the drip pan under the chicken. Close the lid and cook until the chicken reaches 160°F in the thickest part of the breast, about 1 hour.

4. Serve

Remove the chicken from the rotisserie spit and then remove the trussing twine. Be careful — the spit and forks are blazing hot. Let the chicken rest for 15 minutes, then carve and serve.

Notes

- Za'atar usually has some salt in the mix, but not a lot. Check the package; if salt is the first ingredient on the list, skip the salt in the recipe. If it's second (or later) ingredient on the list, add the 1/2 tablespoon of kosher salt listed in the recipe.

SPICE RUBS

Now it's to move past store bought spice blends and make our own.

Why bother mixing your own spice rubs?

It's cheaper — most store bought rubs are mainly salt, and salt is cheap. If you make your own rubs, you're only paying spice prices for the spices in the rub.

You control the salt level — you don't have to worry about how much salt is in the rub. I mix up big batches of my spice rubs without adding any salt. That way, I can salt the chicken however I want; I can wet brine the bird ahead of time or add salt to the rub at the last minute.

You can adjust the rub — Want it hotter? Add more cayenne. Prefer oregano to thyme? Double up on one, and drop the other. No ancho chile powder available? Go with paprika. Or, even better, smoked paprika…yum.

Feel free to play with the recipes in this chapter. None of them are set in stone; use them as a basic idea, and modify them to your taste. Soon you'll have your own personal spice blends. (One year I gave jars of Mike's Barbecue Rub to all my friends for Christmas.)

One more spice blend tip: spices are cheaper in the bulk aisle of your grocery store. Check there first before buying the little jars in the baking aisle.

Cajun Rub Chicken

Back when I was a teenager, Cajun Cooking exploded on the scene. Justin Wilson took off as the Cajun Chef on PBS (I gar-on-tee it!), and Paul Prudhomme's blackened redfish was everywhere. I found out that "American Cooking" wasn't a single thing — there are regional American cuisines, and they're fantastic. So, this rub is a sentimental favorite.

I use Cajun Spice Rub as an all-purpose seasoning. It's great on fish, pork, and as a flavoring in red beans and rice and jambalaya. And, of course, it makes a superb chicken. Whoo-ie, that's good eatin'!

Ingredients
- 1 (4 pound) chicken

Cajun Spice Rub
- 1 tablespoon kosher salt

- 1 teaspoon paprika
- 1 teaspoon granulated garlic (or garlic powder)
- 1/2 teaspoon granulated onion (or onion powder)
- 1/2 teaspoon fresh ground black pepper
- 1/2 teaspoon dried oregano
- 1/2 teaspoons dried thyme
- 1/4 teaspoon cayenne pepper

1. Rub the chicken

Mix the Cajun Spice Rub ingredients in a small bowl. Sprinkle the chicken with the rub, inside and out, patting it onto the chicken to help it stick. Gently work your fingers between the skin and the breast, then rub some of the spices directly onto the breast meat. Fold the wingtips under the wings and truss the chicken. Skewer the chicken on the rotisserie spit, securing it with the spit forks. Let the chicken rest at room temperature until the grill is ready.

2. Set the grill for indirect high heat

Set up the grill for indirect high heat with the drip pan in the middle of the grill.

3. Rotisserie the chicken

Put the spit on the grill, start the motor spinning, and center the drip pan under the chicken. Close the lid and cook until the chicken reaches 160°F in the thickest part of the breast, about 1 hour.

4. Serve

Remove the chicken from the rotisserie spit and then remove the trussing twine. Be careful — the spit and forks are blazing hot. Let the chicken rest for 15 minutes, then carve and serve.

MEXICAN SPICE RUB CHICKEN

Mexican spices — especially ground chili peppers — make for a fantastic rub. I spent a week in Oaxaca, Mexico with chef Susana Trilling at the Seasons of My Heart cooking school. She recommends a blend of three types of chiles — fruity, smoky, and hot.

I'm using ancho for the fruity flavor, guajillo for the smoky flavor, and chipotle for both smoke and heat. Guajillo peppers can be hard to find outside of Mexican markets; they're worth the effort to track them down. But, If you can't find guajillo, peppers, substitute more ancho powder.

If you go to your Mexican market, and find whole dried peppers, you can grind them yourself. You'll want half an ancho pepper, one whole guajillo, and one whole chipotle for this recipe. Stem and seed the peppers, then toast them on a dry skillet for about a minute, until they turn color slightly. Grind the toasted peppers to a powder in your spice grinder. (I use a coffee grinder that I save for grinding spices.)

Ingredients
- 1 (4 pound) chicken

Mexican Spice Rub
- 1 tablespoon kosher salt
- 1 teaspoon ground ancho chile pepper
- 1 teaspoon ground guajillo chile pepper
- 1 teaspoon garlic powder
- 1/2 teaspoon dried oregano (preferably Mexican oregano)
- 1/2 teaspoon ground chipotle pepper

1. Rub the chicken
Mix the Mexican Spice Rub ingredients in a small bowl. Sprinkle the chicken with the rub, inside and out, patting it onto the chicken to help it stick. Gently work your fingers between the skin and the breast, then rub some of the spices directly onto the breast meat. Fold the wingtips under the wings and truss the chicken. Skewer the chicken on the rotisserie spit, securing it with the spit forks. Let the chicken rest at room temperature until the grill is ready.

2. Set the grill for indirect high heat
Set up the grill for indirect high heat with the drip pan in the middle of the grill.

3. Rotisserie the chicken
Put the spit on the grill, start the motor spinning, and center the drip pan under the chicken. Close the lid and cook until the chicken reaches 160°F in the thickest part of the breast, about 1 hour.

4. Serve
Remove the chicken from the rotisserie spit and then remove the trussing twine. Be careful — the spit and forks are blazing hot. Let the chicken rest for 15 minutes, then carve and serve.

Moroccan Spice Rub Chicken

The Spice Route stretched from India to North Africa, bringing spices to Europe. Ships brought the spices from the Spice Islands, up the Red Sea, and landed in Egypt. Caravans of camels crossed the deserts of North Africa, and Morocco was the last stop before the spices crossed over to Spain. Morocco became famous for their spice markets, and the complex blend of spices they use in their own cuisine.

Ras El Hanout means "head of the shop" in Arabic - each Moroccan spice shop mixes its own signature blend of Ras El Hanout, showing off the best spices they have to offer.

Ingredients
- 1 (4 pound) chicken

Moroccan Spice Rub
- 1 tablespoon kosher salt

- 1 teaspoon ground cumin
- 1 teaspoon ground coriander
- 1 teaspoon sweet paprika
- 1/2 teaspoon fresh ground black pepper
- 1/2 teaspoon turmeric
- 1/2 teaspoon cinnamon
- 1/4 teaspoon allspice

1. Rub the chicken
Mix the Moroccan Spice Rub ingredients in a small bowl. Sprinkle the chicken with the rub, inside and out, patting it onto the chicken to help it stick. Gently work your fingers between the skin and the breast, then rub some of the spices directly onto the breast meat. Fold the wingtips under the wings and truss the chicken. Skewer the chicken on the rotisserie spit, securing it with the spit forks. Let the chicken rest at room temperature until the grill is ready.

2. Set the grill for indirect high heat
Set up the grill for indirect high heat with the drip pan in the middle of the grill.

3. Rotisserie the chicken
Put the spit on the grill, start the motor spinning, and center the drip pan under the chicken. Close the lid and cook until the chicken reaches 160°F in the thickest part of the breast, about 1 hour.

4. Serve
Remove the chicken from the rotisserie spit and then remove the trussing twine. Be careful — the spit and forks are blazing hot. Let the chicken rest for 15 minutes, then carve and serve.

French Four Spices Chicken (Poulet Quatre Epices)

Quatre epices, "four spices" in French, is a common spice blend in French kitchens. (It usually has five spices in it — go figure.)

Quatre epices started as a seasoning for sausages and pâtés, but is now used on a variety of foods in the French kitchen, including roasted meats. For example, this poulet rôti, a fabulous French roast chicken.

Ingredients
- 1 (4 pound) chicken

Quatre Epices Spice Rub
- 1 tablespoon kosher salt
- 1 teaspoon fresh ground white pepper (or substitute black pepper, or a peppercorn blend)

- 1/2 teaspoon ground ginger
- 1/2 teaspoon ground cinnamon
- 1/2 teaspoon freshly grated nutmeg
- 1/4 teaspoon ground cloves

1. Rub the chicken

Mix the Quatre Epices Spice Rub ingredients in a small bowl. Sprinkle the chicken with the rub, inside and out, patting it onto the chicken to help it stick. Gently work your fingers between the skin and the breast, then rub some of the spices directly onto the breast meat. Fold the wingtips under the wings and truss the chicken. Skewer the chicken on the rotisserie spit, securing it with the spit forks. Let the chicken rest at room temperature until the grill is ready.

2. Set the grill for indirect high heat

Set up the grill for indirect high heat with the drip pan in the middle of the grill.

3. Rotisserie the chicken

Put the spit on the grill, start the motor spinning, and center the drip pan under the chicken. Close the lid and cook until the chicken reaches 160°F in the thickest part of the breast, about 1 hour.

4. Serve

Remove the chicken from the rotisserie spit and then remove the trussing twine. Be careful — the spit and forks are blazing hot. Let the chicken rest for 15 minutes, then carve and serve.

Pastrami Rub Chicken

My favorite deli order is a pastrami on rye, with mustard and horseradish. (And, if I'm really lucky, they'll have chopped chicken liver to spread on as well.)

I love the peppery, spicy crust on pastrami — so much that I'll also use it on chicken. And, of course, leftovers make a great sandwich, sliced thin and served on rye, with mustard and…well, you know the rest.

Ingredients
- 1 (4 pound) chicken

Pastrami spice rub
- 1 tablespoon kosher salt
- 1 teaspoon coarse ground black pepper
- 1 teaspoon coarse ground coriander seed

- 1/2 teaspoon garlic powder
- 1/2 teaspoon brown sugar

1. Rub the chicken
Mix the Pastrami Spice Rub ingredients in a small bowl. Sprinkle the chicken with the rub, inside and out, patting it onto the chicken to help it stick. Gently work your fingers between the skin and the breast, then rub some of the spices directly onto the breast meat. Fold the wingtips under the wings and truss the chicken. Skewer the chicken on the rotisserie spit, securing it with the spit forks. Let the chicken rest at room temperature until the grill is ready.

2. Set the grill for indirect high heat
Set up the grill for indirect high heat with the drip pan in the middle of the grill.

3. Rotisserie the chicken
Put the spit on the grill, start the motor spinning, and center the drip pan under the chicken. Close the lid and cook until the chicken reaches 160°F in the thickest part of the breast, about 1 hour.

4. Serve
Remove the chicken from the rotisserie spit and then remove the trussing twine. Be careful — the spit and forks are blazing hot. Let the chicken rest for 15 minutes, then carve and serve.

BARBECUED BIRDS

Barbecue. Depending on where you go, it can be something to eat (let's have some barbecue), something to do (time to barbecue the chicken), somewhere to go (we'll meet at the barbecue), or something to cook on (I'll put the chicken on the barbecue). Or, it can be all of them at once: Let's go to the barbecue and eat barbecue, barbecued on the barbecue. I don't mind if I do.

It is time to tour the Barbecue Belt, from the Carolinas in the East to Texas in the West, stopping in Kansas City, Memphis, and Alabama along the way.

Most of these barbecue regions have a signature meat…and it usually isn't chicken. Pork wins out in the East and Midwest, and beef is king in Texas, but every barbecue joint I've been in also has chicken on the menu. They figure, "We already have the pit fired up, why not put a chicken in there?"

Alabama is the notable exception — their white barbecue sauce is made specifically for chicken.

There's a reason everyone makes barbecued chicken; chicken, wood smoke, and barbecue sauce just go together.

Now, for some cooking notes:

I cook my barbecued birds at medium heat, not the high heat I use on most chickens. Barbecue rub usually has sugar in it; the lower heat to keep it from burning in the grill. I save the barbecue sauce for a last minute glaze for the same reason — barbecue sauce has a lot of sugar, and if it's on the grill for too long, it will burn. I try to get two or three coats of sauce on the bird during the last fifteen minutes — the heat of the grill tightens up the sauce into layers of caramelized glaze, adding even more complexity to the barbecue flavors.

Kansas City BBQ Chicken

The barbecued chicken of my youth was dunked in a thick, sweet barbecue sauce, and then thrown on the grill. The result? Chicken that was burnt and blackened on the outside, with bloody, undercooked meat near the bone. That thick sweet sauce was the culprit — barbecue sauce will burn long before the chicken is cooked through if you grill it over direct heat.

I still loved that chicken. (Hey, I'm a Northerner. What did I know?)

Since then, I've learned my barbecue lessons: indirect heat, lower temperatures, smoking wood, and a barbecue rub to add an extra layer of flavor. This is barbecued chicken I could only dream of as a kid.

Ingredients
- 1 (4 pound) chicken

- Smoking wood, preferably hickory. A fist sized chunk for a charcoal grill or 1 cup of wood chips for a gas grill

Kansas City Barbecue Rub
- 1 tablespoon kosher salt
- 1 tablespoon sweet paprika
- 1 teaspoon brown sugar
- 1 teaspoon chili powder blend
- 1 teaspoon garlic powder
- 1 teaspoon onion powder
- 1/2 teaspoon cayenne pepper

Kansas City Barbecue Sauce
- 1 cup ketchup
- 1/4 cup brown sugar
- 1/4 cup molasses
- 1/4 cup cider vinegar
- 1 teaspoon reserved barbecue rub

1. Season, truss and spit the chicken

Mix the Kansas City Barbecue Rub ingredients in a small bowl. Reserve 1 teaspoon of the rub for the barbecue sauce, then sprinkle the chicken with the rest of the rub, inside and out, patting it onto the chicken to help it stick. Gently work your fingers between the skin and the breast, then rub some of the barbecue rub directly onto the breast meat. Fold the wingtips under the wings and truss the chicken. Skewer the chicken on the rotisserie spit, securing it with the spit forks. Let the chicken rest at room temperature until the grill is ready. Submerge the smoking wood in water and let it soak until the grill is ready.

2. Set the grill for indirect medium heat

Set up the grill for indirect medium heat with the drip pan in the middle of the grill.

3. Make the barbecue sauce

Whisk the Kansas City Barbecue Sauce ingredients in a small saucepan. Bring the sauce to a simmer over medium heat, simmer for five minutes, then remove from the heat and save for later.

4. Rotisserie the chicken

Put the spit on the grill, start the motor spinning, and center the drip pan under the chicken. Add the smoking wood to the fire, close the lid, and cook until the chicken reaches 160°F in the thickest part of the breast, about 1 hour and 15 minutes. During the last fifteen minutes of cooking, brush the chicken with a layer of barbecue sauce every five minutes.

5. Serve

Remove the chicken from the rotisserie spit and then remove the trussing twine. Be careful — the spit and forks are blazing hot. Brush with one last coat of sauce, then let the chicken rest for 15 minutes. Carve and serve, passing the remaining barbecue sauce at the table.

Memphis Dry Rub Chicken

Most places have a single style of barbecue, which the locals defend as the One True Style of barbecue. Memphis, Tennessee is the outlier; they have two local styles. The question is: "Wet or dry?" Do you want your 'que wet — coated in sauce? Or do you want it dry, dusted with barbecue rub?

Here's my take on dry barbecue. Dry ribs are the specialty at Charlie Vergos' Rendezvous restaurant, but of course, they also use their signature rub on chicken. If you can't make it to the Rendezvous in Memphis, mix up a batch of this rub, and try it dry in your own back yard.

Ingredients
- 1 (4 pound) chicken
- Smoking wood, preferably hickory. A fist sized chunk for a charcoal grill or 1 cup of wood chips for a gas grill

Memphis Dry Rub
- 1 tablespoon kosher salt
- 2 teaspoons paprika
- 1 teaspoon granulated garlic (or garlic powder)
- 1/2 teaspoon fresh ground black pepper
- 1/2 teaspoon ground coriander
- 1/2 teaspoon yellow mustard powder
- 1/2 teaspoon dried oregano
- 1/2 teaspoons dried thyme
- 1/4 teaspoon cayenne pepper

1. Rub the chicken
Mix the Memphis Dry Rub ingredients in a small bowl. Sprinkle the chicken with the rub, inside and out, patting it onto the chicken to help it stick. Gently work your fingers between the skin and the breast, then rub some of the spices directly onto the breast meat. Fold the wingtips under the wings and truss the chicken. Skewer the chicken on the rotisserie spit, securing it with the spit forks. Let the chicken rest at room temperature until the grill is ready. Submerge the smoking wood in water and let it soak until the grill is ready.

2. Set the grill for indirect medium heat
Set up the grill for indirect medium heat with the drip pan in the middle of the grill.

3. Rotisserie the chicken
Put the spit on the grill, start the motor spinning, and center the drip pan under the chicken. Add the smoking wood to the fire, close the lid, and cook until the chicken reaches 160°F in the thickest part of the breast, about 1 hour and 15 minutes.

4. Serve
Remove the chicken from the rotisserie spit and then remove the trussing twine. Be careful — the spit and forks are blazing hot. Let the chicken rest for 15 minutes, then carve and serve.

South Carolina Golden Mustard BBQ Chicken

Pulled pork with mustard based barbecue sauce is the state barbecue of South Carolina. And, shh…don't tell anyone, but this is my favorite barbecue sauce.

<Ducks and hides behind computer screen, waiting for angry mob of barbecue fanatics to form. After a few seconds, pokes his head up, looks around, and continues…>

The sauce may be intended for pork, but mustard and chicken are a classic combination. I use this sauce with chicken all the time — probably more often than I do with pork.

My favorite Carolina Gold sauce comes from Duke's Barbecue in Walterboro, South Carolina. I prefer their rusty red "Hot" style sauce, with a kick of spicy peppers. I add Tabasco sauce to bring the heat, but you can use your favorite hot sauce, or skip the hot sauce altogether for a milder barbecued chicken.

Ingredients
- 1 (4 pound) chicken
- Smoking wood, preferably hickory. A fist sized chunk for a charcoal grill or 1 cup of wood chips for a gas grill

Barbecue Rub
- 1 tablespoon kosher salt
- 2 teaspoons sweet paprika
- 1 teaspoon brown sugar
- 1 teaspoon yellow mustard powder
- 1 teaspoon garlic powder

South Carolina Gold Barbecue Sauce
- 1 cup yellow mustard
- 1/2 cup brown sugar
- 1/4 cup cider vinegar
- 1/4 cup ketchup
- 1 tablespoon soy sauce
- 1 tablespoon Worcestershire sauce
- 1 tablespoon hot sauce (optional. I use Tabasco sauce.)
- 1 teaspoon reserved barbecue rub

1. Season, truss and spit the chicken

Mix the barbecue rub ingredients in a small bowl. Reserve 1 teaspoon of the rub for the barbecue sauce, then sprinkle the chicken with the rest of the rub, inside and out, patting it onto the chicken to help it stick. Gently work your fingers between the skin and the breast, then rub some of the barbecue rub directly onto the breast meat. Fold the wingtips under the wings and truss the chicken. Skewer the chicken on the rotisserie spit, securing it with the spit forks. Let the chicken rest at room temperature until the grill is ready. Submerge the smoking wood in water and let it soak until the grill is ready.

2. Set the grill for indirect medium heat

Set up the grill for indirect medium heat with the drip pan in the middle of the grill.

3. Make the barbecue sauce

Whisk the South Carolina Gold Barbecue Sauce ingredients in a small bowl until the brown sugar dissolves.

4. Rotisserie the chicken

Put the spit on the grill, start the motor spinning, and center the drip pan under the chicken. Add the smoking wood to the fire, close the lid, and cook until the chicken reaches 160°F in the thickest part of the breast, about 1 hour and 15 minutes. During the last fifteen minutes of cooking, brush the chicken with a layer of barbecue sauce every five minutes.

5. Serve

Remove the chicken from the rotisserie spit and then remove the trussing twine. Be careful — the spit and forks are blazing hot. Brush with one last coat of sauce, then let the chicken rest for 15 minutes. Carve and serve, passing the remaining barbecue sauce at the table.

Texas BBQ Chicken

I get in trouble when I write about Texas. At least one person will respond with: "well, that may taste good where *you* come from, but we do it different down here. Don't mess with Texas."

I did extra research for this book, determined to get it right this time. I ate my way across Austin, hopping from barbecue joint to barbecue joint. (That counts as research, right?) In between the brisket, short ribs, and turkey, I ate a lot of chicken. It was smoked over oak, sprinkled with a simple rub with a hint of heat. On the side was a thin barbecue sauce, heavy on Worcestershire and black pepper.

Here's my version of Texas barbecued chicken, crisped up and glazed on the rotisserie. I'm sorry, I can't help messing with Texas.

Ingredients
- 1 (4 pound) chicken
- Smoking wood, preferably oak. A fist sized chunk for a

charcoal grill or 1 cup of wood chips for a gas grill

Barbecue Rub
- 1 tablespoon kosher salt
- 1 tablespoon ground ancho chile pepper
- 1 teaspoon ground cumin
- 1 teaspoon fresh ground black pepper

Texas Barbecue Sauce
- 3/4 cup ketchup
- 1/4 cup Worcestershire sauce
- 1/4 cup cider vinegar
- 2 tablespoons brown sugar
- 1 teaspoon fresh ground black pepper
- 1/2 teaspoon cayenne pepper
- 1 teaspoon reserved barbecue rub

1. Season, truss and spit the chicken

Mix the barbecue rub ingredients in a small bowl. Reserve 1 teaspoon of the rub for the barbecue sauce, then sprinkle the chicken with the rest of the rub, inside and out, patting it onto the chicken to help it stick. Gently work your fingers between the skin and the breast, then rub some of the barbecue rub directly onto the breast meat. Fold the wingtips under the wings and truss the chicken. Skewer the chicken on the rotisserie spit, securing it with the spit forks. Let the chicken rest at room temperature until the grill is ready. Submerge the smoking wood in water and let it soak until the grill is ready.

2. Set the grill for indirect medium heat

Set up the grill for indirect medium heat with the drip pan in the middle of the grill.

3. Make the barbecue sauce

Whisk the Texas Barbecue Sauce ingredients in a small saucepan. Bring the sauce to a simmer over medium heat, simmer for five minutes, then remove from the heat and save for later.

4. Rotisserie the chicken

Put the spit on the grill, start the motor spinning, and center the drip pan under the chicken. Add the smoking wood to the fire, close the lid, and cook until the chicken reaches 160°F in the thickest part of the breast, about 1 hour and 15 minutes. During the last fifteen minutes of cooking, brush the chicken with a layer of barbecue sauce every five minutes.

5. Serve

Remove the chicken from the rotisserie spit and then remove the trussing twine. Be careful — the spit and forks are blazing hot. Brush with one last coat of sauce, then let the chicken rest for 15 minutes. Carve and serve, passing the remaining barbecue sauce at the table.

Alabama White BBQ Chicken

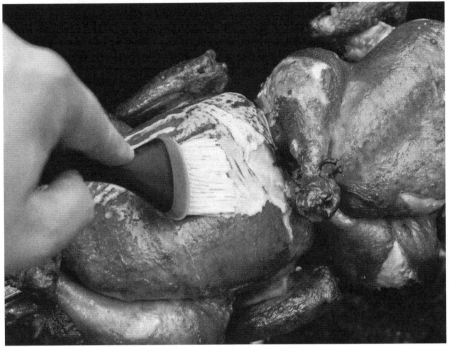

White barbecue sauce? White barbecue sauce. It's a specialty of Decatur, Alabama, invented in the 1920's at Big Bob Gibson's Bar-B-Q. And, unlike most barbecue sauces, it is meant to be used on chicken!

Alabama chicken is barbecued in a hickory smoker, and finished with a dunk in a big pot of white sauce. White sauce is for more than just for barbecued chicken; In Alabama, it is an all-purpose condiment. It is used as a table sauce, a salad dressing, and to top everything from pork to fish. (I particularly love it for dipping potato chips.)

Ingredients
- 1 (4 pound) chicken
- Smoking wood, preferably hickory. A fist sized chunk for a charcoal grill or 1 cup of wood chips for a gas grill

Barbecue Rub

- 1 tablespoon kosher salt
- 1 teaspoon brown sugar
- 1/2 teaspoon yellow mustard powder
- 1/2 teaspoon garlic powder
- 1/2 teaspoon onion powder
- 1/2 teaspoon fresh ground black pepper

Alabama White Barbecue Sauce
- 1 cup mayonnaise
- 1/4 cup apple cider vinegar
- 1/4 cup brown sugar
- 1 teaspoons fresh ground black pepper
- 1/4 teaspoon cayenne pepper
- 1 teaspoon reserved barbecue rub

1. Season, truss and spit the chicken
Mix the barbecue rub ingredients in a small bowl. Reserve 1 teaspoon of the rub for the barbecue sauce, then sprinkle the chicken with the rest of the rub, inside and out, patting it onto the chicken to help it stick. Gently work your fingers between the skin and the breast, then rub some of the barbecue rub directly onto the breast meat. Fold the wingtips under the wings and truss the chicken. Skewer the chicken on the rotisserie spit, securing it with the spit forks. Let the chicken rest at room temperature until the grill is ready. Submerge the smoking wood in water and let it soak until the grill is ready.

2. Set the grill for indirect medium heat
Set up the grill for indirect medium heat with the drip pan in the middle of the grill.

3. Make the barbecue sauce
Whisk the barbecue sauce ingredients in a small bowl until the brown sugar dissolves.

4. Rotisserie the chicken
Put the spit on the grill, start the motor spinning, and center the drip

pan under the chicken. Add the smoking wood to the fire, close the lid, and cook until the chicken reaches 160°F in the thickest part of the breast, about 1 hour and 15 minutes. During the last fifteen minutes of cooking, brush the chicken with a layer of barbecue sauce every five minutes.

5. Serve

Remove the chicken from the rotisserie spit and then remove the trussing twine. Be careful — the spit and forks are blazing hot. Brush with one last coat of sauce, then let the chicken rest for 15 minutes. Carve and serve, passing the remaining barbecue sauce at the table.

Liquored Up

Why use alcohol in cooking? It's not just to lubricate the cook... though I don't mind that side effect.

A lot of flavors are alcohol soluble, and only come out when a bit of booze is added. Think of vodka and cream sauce — it tastes so good because the alcohol in the vodka perks up the flavor of the tomatoes.

Now, my goal is NOT to get everyone at the dinner table drunk. These sauces need to simmer before they go on the chicken, which boils away the harsh flavor of the alcohol. Simmering also helps the sauce thicken into a glaze — I want the sauce to stick to the chicken instead of dripping off into the pan.

Like the barbecue sauces in the previous chapter, these glazes have sugar in them, and will burn in the heat of the grill. I brush them on during the last fifteen minutes of cooking.

Another common theme is pairing liquor and fruit. Fruit and liquor are an awesome combination. These recipes are based on classic fruity drinks, like margaritas, whiskey sours, and tequila sunrises. (Which makes it obvious what you should drink with the chicken.)

Now, please, this is not the time to use top shelf bottles. Save the single malt scotch, 18 year Irish whiskey, single barrel bourbon, or añejo tequila for sipping, and use cheap(er) liquor for cooking.

Don't want to use alcohol? Substitute a quarter cup of chicken stock and a teaspoon of cider vinegar. It won't bring out the flavors quite as much — remember the alcohol solubility — but it adds body and acid to the sauce, making up for the missing liquor.

BOURBON AND MAPLE SYRUP CHICKEN

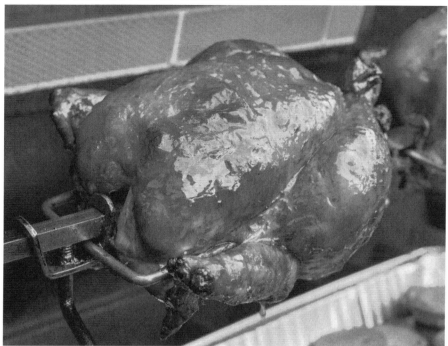

Bourbon is the classic American whiskey, made up of at least 51% corn mash and aged in charred oak barrels. This recipe builds on the smoky oak and sweet corn flavors of bourbon with smoking wood and maple syrup. Then I add a splash of balsamic vinegar; the hint of tart vinegar balances out the smoky, sweet profile of the glaze.

So, what should you drink with this chicken? A **Maple Old Fashioned**: Pour 2 ounces of bourbon and 1/2 an ounce of maple syrup into a rocks glass. Add 2 to 3 dashes of bitters. Fill with ice, top off with club soda, and stir. Serve with a slice of orange. Makes 1 drink.

Ingredients
- 1 (4 pound) chicken
- 1 tablespoon kosher salt
- 1/2 teaspoon fresh ground black pepper

- Smoking wood, preferably oak. A fist sized chunk for a charcoal grill or 1 cup of wood chips for a gas grill

Bourbon and Maple Syrup Glaze
- 1/4 cup bourbon
- 1/4 maple syrup
- 2 tablespoons balsamic vinegar

1. Season, truss and spit the chicken
Season the chicken with the salt and pepper, inside and out. Gently work your fingers between the skin and the breast, then rub some of the salt directly onto the breast meat. Fold the wingtips under the wings and truss the chicken. Skewer the chicken on the rotisserie spit, securing it with the spit forks. Let the chicken rest at room temperature until the grill is ready.

2. Set the grill for indirect high heat
Set up the grill for indirect high heat with the drip pan in the middle of the grill.

3. Make the glaze
Whisk the Bourbon Brown Sugar glaze ingredients in a small saucepan. Simmer over medium heat until the sauce thickens into a glaze, about five minutes. Remove from the heat and set aside for later.

4. Rotisserie the chicken
Put the spit on the grill, start the motor spinning, and center the drip pan under the chicken. Add the smoking wood to the fire, close the lid, and cook until the chicken reaches 160°F in the thickest part of the breast, about 1 hour. During the last fifteen minutes of cooking, brush the chicken with a layer of glaze every five minutes.

5. Serve
Remove the chicken from the rotisserie spit and then remove the trussing twine. Be careful — the spit and forks are blazing hot. Brush

the chicken with one last coat of glaze, then let it rest for 15 minutes. Carve, drizzle with any remaining glaze, and serve.

Tequila Lime Chicken

Tequila is made from the heart of the blue agave plant in Jalisco, Mexico. (If it's not from Jalisco, it may be good, it's not Tequila.) Think of this recipe as a margarita glaze — sweet, tequila, and lime, brushed on the chicken. I use agave syrup in the glaze; it seems like the obvious choice to pair with agave based tequila.

So, what should you drink with this chicken? A pitcher of **Frozen Margaritas**: Put 4 cups of ice, 6 ounces of frozen limeade concentrate, the juice of 1 lime, 1/2 cup of tequila, and 1/4 cup of triple sec in a blender. Blend until frosty, pour into salt-rimmed glasses, and serve. Makes 4 margaritas; 2 if you use jumbo margarita glasses.

Ingredients
- 1 (4 pound) chicken
- 1 tablespoon kosher salt

- 1/2 teaspoon fresh ground black pepper

Tequila Lime Glaze
- 1/4 cup tequila
- 1/4 cup fresh squeezed lime juice (juice of 2 limes)
- 1/4 cup agave syrup (or substitute honey)

1. Season, truss and spit the chicken
Season the chicken with the salt and pepper, inside and out. Gently work your fingers between the skin and the breast, then rub some of the salt directly onto the breast meat. Fold the wingtips under the wings and truss the chicken. Skewer the chicken on the rotisserie spit, securing it with the spit forks.

2. Set the grill for indirect high heat
Set up the grill for indirect high heat with the drip pan in the middle of the grill.

3. Make the glaze
Whisk the tequila lime glaze ingredients in a small saucepan. Simmer over medium heat until the sauce thickens into a glaze, about five minutes. Remove from the heat and set aside for later.

4. Rotisserie the chicken
Put the spit on the grill, start the motor spinning, and center the drip pan under the chicken. Close the lid and cook until the chicken reaches 160°F in the thickest part of the breast, about 1 hour. During the last fifteen minutes of cooking, brush the chicken with a layer of glaze every five minutes.

5. Serve
Remove the chicken from the rotisserie spit and then remove the trussing twine. Be careful — the spit and forks are blazing hot. Brush the chicken with one last coat of glaze, then let it rest for 15 minutes. Carve, drizzle with any remaining glaze, and serve.

Mezcal Sunrise Chicken

With apologies to Glen Frey: Not another tequila sunrise - it's a mezcal sunrise.

I fell in love with mezcal on my trip to Oaxaca, where they make it from the smoke-roasted heart of the maguey plant. Tequila and mezcal are related — tequila is a specific type of mezcal, and maguey is a relative of agave. Sweet, smoky mezcal adds an extra dimension of flavor to this drinks that normally use tequila.

So, while we're talking mezcal…what's the deal with the worm in the mezcal bottle? Gusano rojo worms are attracted to the sweet sap of the maguey plant. Allegedly, a gusano rojo worm in the bottle adds flavor to the mezcal. I'm not buying it — I think the worm is a marketing ploy. None of the high end brands of mezcal I tried in Oaxaca had a worm floating in them, and they were fantastic.

What should you drink with this chicken? A **Mezcal Sunrise**: Pour 2 ounces of tequila into a highball glass, then top off with orange juice. Carefully pour 1/2 ounce of grenadine syrup down the inside of the glass; you want it to settle to the bottom. Add a slice of orange and serve. Makes 1 drink.

Ingredients
- 1 (4 pound) chicken
- 1 tablespoon kosher salt
- 1/2 teaspoon fresh ground black pepper

Mezcal Sunrise Glaze
- 1/4 cup mezcal (or substitute tequila)
- 1/4 cup orange juice
- 1 tablespoon grenadine syrup

1. Season, truss and spit the chicken
Season the chicken with the salt and pepper, inside and out. Gently work your fingers between the skin and the breast, then rub some of the salt directly onto the breast meat. Fold the wingtips under the wings and truss the chicken. Skewer the chicken on the rotisserie spit, securing it with the spit forks. Drive a long, thin knife through the middle of the pineapple to make a pilot hole, then push the pineapple onto the spit, and secure it with another spit fork. Let the chicken and pineapple rest at room temperature until the grill is ready.

2. Set the grill for indirect high heat
Set up the grill for indirect high heat with the drip pan in the middle of the grill.

3. Make the glaze
Whisk the tequila sunrise glaze ingredients in a small saucepan. Simmer over medium heat until the sauce thickens into a glaze, about five minutes. Remove from the heat and set aside for later.

4. Rotisserie the chicken

Put the spit on the grill, start the motor spinning, and center the drip pan under the chicken. Add the smoking wood to the fire, close the lid, and cook until the chicken reaches 160°F in the thickest part of the breast, about 1 hour. During the last fifteen minutes of cooking, brush the chicken with a layer of glaze every five minutes.

5. Serve
Remove the chicken from the rotisserie spit and then remove the trussing twine. Be careful — the spit and forks are blazing hot. Brush the chicken with one last coat of glaze, then let it rest for 15 minutes. Carve, drizzle with any remaining glaze, and serve.

POMEGRANATE GIN CHICKEN

I've made pomegranate glazed birds before, so when I read about pomegranate gin fizz cocktails, it caught my attention. Spicy gin and pomegranate juice? I had to try it — as a glaze.

Yes, I'm strange that way. I didn't want a drink, I wanted a chicken glaze.

Well, OK, I did have to try the drink as well. Just as a test, mind you.

Now, the ideal sweetener for this glaze is pomegranate molasses. It's hard to come by in my neck of the woods; I can only find it online. So, I use pomegranate juice and honey, and simmer it down to thicken the glaze. If you can find pomegranate molasses, substitute it for the pomegranate juice, skip the honey, and cut back on the simmering time — thicker pomegranate molasses needs less time to turn into a glaze.

So, what should you drink with this chicken? A **Pomegranate Gin Fizz**: Shake ice, 2 ounces of gin, and 1/2 ounce of pomegranate liqueur in a cocktail shaker, and strain into a highball glass. Fill the glass with ice and top with soda water. Makes 1 drink.

Ingredients
- 1 (4 pound) chicken
- 1 tablespoon kosher salt
- 1/2 teaspoon fresh ground black pepper

Pomegranate Gin Glaze
- 1/4 cup gin
- 1/4 cup pomegranate juice
- 2 tablespoons honey

1. Season, truss and spit the chicken
Season the chicken with the salt and pepper, inside and out. Gently work your fingers between the skin and the breast, then rub some of the salt directly onto the breast meat. Fold the wingtips under the wings and truss the chicken. Skewer the chicken on the rotisserie spit, securing it with the spit forks.

2. Set the grill for indirect high heat
Set up the grill for indirect high heat with the drip pan in the middle of the grill.

3. Make the glaze
Whisk the pomegranate gin glaze ingredients in a small saucepan. Simmer over medium heat until the sauce thickens into a glaze, about five minutes. Remove from the heat and set aside for later.

4. Rotisserie the chicken
Put the spit on the grill, start the motor spinning, and center the drip pan under the chicken. Close the lid and cook until the chicken reaches 160°F in the thickest part of the breast, about 1 hour. During

the last fifteen minutes of cooking, brush the chicken with a layer of glaze every five minutes.

5. Serve

Remove the chicken from the rotisserie spit and then remove the trussing twine. Brush the chicken with one last coat of glaze, then let it rest for 15 minutes. Carve, drizzle with any remaining glaze, and serve.

WHISKEY SOUR CHICKEN

I'm sure you have noticed a theme to my Liquored Up recipes; each glaze has sweet and sour components to balance out the complex flavors of alcohol.

A Whiskey Sour is already a balance of sweet, sour and liquor; it's practically designed to be one of my chicken glazes. Just about any variety of whiskey will work here; Bourbon, Scotch, Irish, Canadian… whatever you have on hand will do the trick.

So, what should you drink with this chicken? A **Whiskey Sour**: Shake ice, 2 ounces of whiskey, 1 ounce of lemon juice, and 1 ounce of simple syrup in a cocktail shaker, and strain into a rocks glass. Fill the glass with ice and top with a slice of lemon. Makes 1 drink.

Ingredients
- 1 (4 pound) chicken
- 1 tablespoon kosher salt

- 1/2 teaspoon fresh ground black pepper

Whiskey Sour Glaze
- 1/4 cup whiskey
- 1/4 cup fresh squeezed lime juice (juice of 2 limes)
- 2 tablespoons brown sugar
- 1/2 teaspoon fresh ground black pepper

1. Season, truss and spit the chicken
Season the chicken with the salt and pepper, inside and out. Gently work your fingers between the skin and the breast, then rub some of the salt directly onto the breast meat. Fold the wingtips under the wings and truss the chicken. Skewer the chicken on the rotisserie spit, securing it with the spit forks.

2. Set the grill for indirect high heat
Set up the grill for indirect high heat with the drip pan in the middle of the grill.

3. Make the glaze
Whisk the whiskey sour glaze ingredients in a small saucepan. Simmer over medium heat until the sauce thickens into a glaze, about five minutes. Remove from the heat and set aside for later.

4. Rotisserie the chicken
Put the spit on the grill, start the motor spinning, and center the drip pan under the chicken. Add the smoking wood to the fire, close the lid, and cook until the chicken reaches 160°F in the thickest part of the breast, about 1 hour. During the last fifteen minutes of cooking, brush the chicken with a layer of glaze every five minutes.

5. Serve
Remove the chicken from the rotisserie spit and then remove the trussing twine. Be careful — the spit and forks are blazing hot. Brush the chicken with one last coat of glaze, then let it rest for 15 minutes. Carve, drizzle with any remaining glaze, and serve.

MEDITERRANEAN HERB PASTES

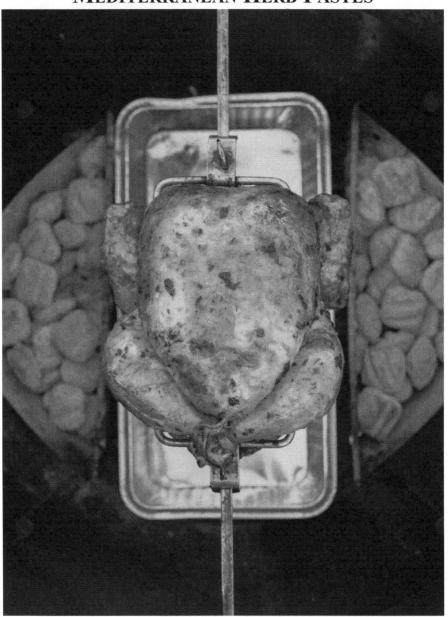

Mediterranean cooking is defined by the set of ingredients that grow along its shores. Olive oil is the backbone, both as a cooking oil and as a garnish. Garlic? You better like garlic if you're going to eat

Mediterranean; it is everywhere. Fresh herbs and citrus all thrive in this sun drenched region, and are an integral part of its cooking.

Next come spices. The countries surrounding the Mediterranean have been players in the spice trade since medieval times. Mediterranean cooking is the original "global fusion cuisine", adopting spices from as far away as India and Indonesia, and integrating them into their recipes.

The recipes in this chapter are olive oil based pastes, thicker than a marinade, wetter than a rub. They all have some garlic, and the herbs, spices, and citrus flavors change as we cross the Mediterranean, from Spain in the West, to the Levant in the East.

Spanish Smoked Paprika and Garlic Chicken

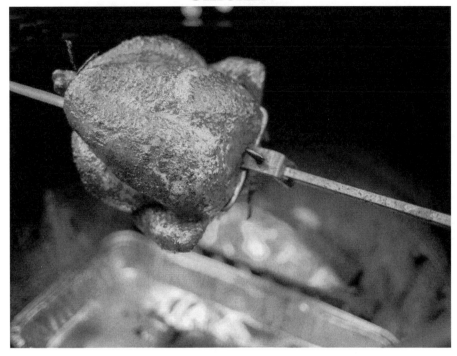

Pimenton De La Vera is Spanish smoked paprika. It has been used in Spain for centuries, but in America it came out of nowhere as a popular ingredient back in the early 2000's. I remember hunting for the small tins, and the excitement of finding the blue and white box with Santo Domingo on the front. Nowadays, it is much easier to find, a common ingredient in the spice aisle of your local grocery store.

This spice paste is perfect for gas rotisserie grilling. The olive oil helps the chicken to brown, and Spanish paprika gives the chicken a layer of smoky flavor, as if it was cooked over charcoal. (But, don't skip it if you have a charcoal grill — it still tastes great!)

Ingredients
- 1 (4 pound) chicken

Spice paste
- 1 tablespoon olive oil
- 1 tablespoon kosher salt
- 1 tablespoon smoked Spanish paprika (Pimenton de la Vera)
- 2 cloves garlic, finely minced
- 1/2 teaspoon fresh thyme
- 1/2 teaspoon freshly ground black pepper

1. Rub the chicken
Mix the spice paste ingredients in a small bowl. Rub the chicken with the paste, inside and out. Gently work your fingers between the skin and the breast, then rub some of the paste directly onto the breast meat. Fold the wingtips under the wings and truss the chicken. Skewer the chicken on the rotisserie spit, securing it with the spit forks. Let the chicken rest at room temperature until the grill is ready.

2. Set the grill for indirect high heat
Set up the grill for indirect high heat with the drip pan in the middle of the grill.

3. Rotisserie the chicken
Put the spit on the grill, start the motor spinning, and center the drip pan under the chicken. Add the smoking wood to the fire, close the lid, and cook until the chicken reaches 160°F in the thickest part of the breast, about 1 hour.

4. Serve
Remove the chicken from the rotisserie spit and then remove the trussing twine. Be careful — the spit and forks are blazing hot. Let the chicken rest for 15 minutes, then carve and serve.

FRENCH FINES HERBES CHICKEN

Fines Herbes are a classic French mix of parsley, tarragon, chervil, and chives, and sometimes marjoram. This herb rubbed rotisserie chicken takes me back to the roti vendor in the Provencal market of L'Isle-sur-la-Sorgue…without the 8 hour trans-Atlantic flight.

I have a hard time finding chervil in my area, so I go with marjoram in my mix. (If you can't find marjoram, use extra parsley.) All the rest of the herbs are easy to find in clamshell packages at my local grocery store, or growing in the herb garden in my front yard, where chives and parsley duel for supremacy each summer.

Ingredients
- 1 (4 pound) chicken

Herb paste
- 1 tablespoon olive oil

- 1 tablespoon kosher salt
- 1 tablespoon minced parsley leaves
- 1 teaspoon minced fresh marjoram
- 1 teaspoon minced fresh tarragon leaves
- 1 teaspoon minced fresh chives
- 1/2 teaspoon freshly ground white pepper (or substitute black pepper)

1. Rub the chicken
Mix the herb paste ingredients in a small bowl. Rub the chicken with the paste, inside and out. Gently work your fingers between the skin and the breast, then rub some of the herbs directly onto the breast meat. Fold the wingtips under the wings and truss the chicken. Skewer the chicken on the rotisserie spit, securing it with the spit forks. Let the chicken rest at room temperature until the grill is ready.

2. Set the grill for indirect high heat
Set up the grill for indirect high heat with the drip pan in the middle of the grill.

3. Rotisserie the chicken
Put the spit on the grill, start the motor spinning, and center the drip pan under the chicken. Close the lid and cook until the chicken reaches 160°F in the thickest part of the breast, about 1 hour.

4. Serve
Remove the chicken from the rotisserie spit and then remove the trussing twine. Be careful — the spit and forks are blazing hot. Let the chicken rest for 15 minutes, then carve and serve.

Italian Black and Red Pepper Chicken

Pollo Alla Diavola, Italian "chicken from the devil", is rubbed with a paste heavy on black and red peppers, giving it a spicy kick. That heat is where the colorful nickname came from…though, as with most culinary history, this is a subject of dispute. Is it "from the devil" because of the spicy crust? Or because of the high heat cooking method? Or both?

Wherever the name came from, this is the chicken for molto piccante food lovers.

Ingredients
- 1 (4 pound) chicken

Spice paste
- 1 tablespoon olive oil
- 1 tablespoon kosher salt

- 1 teaspoon coarsely ground black pepper
- 1 teaspoon crushed red pepper flakes
- Zest of 1 lemon, minced

1. Rub the chicken
Mix the spice paste ingredients in a small bowl. Rub the chicken with the paste, inside and out. Gently work your fingers between the skin and the breast, then rub some of the spices directly onto the breast meat. Fold the wingtips under the wings and truss the chicken. Skewer the chicken on the rotisserie spit, securing it with the spit forks. Let the chicken rest at room temperature until the grill is ready.

2. Set the grill for indirect high heat
Set up the grill for indirect high heat with the drip pan in the middle of the grill.

3. Rotisserie the chicken
Put the spit on the grill, start the motor spinning, and center the drip pan under the chicken. Close the lid and cook until the chicken reaches 160°F in the thickest part of the breast, about 1 hour.

4. Serve
Remove the chicken from the rotisserie spit and then remove the trussing twine. Be careful — the spit and forks are blazing hot. Let the chicken rest for 15 minutes, then carve and serve.

Greek Oregano, Lemon, and Garlic Chicken

In my imagination, I'm on the island of Santorini, staring out over the glittering blue Aegean Sea. In the background, framed by the white towers of a monastery, is a chicken spinning on a spit, rubbed with olive oil, garlic, lemon, and oregano. Opa!

(PS: Head to the drip pan potatoes chapter, and make Yukon Gold Greek Potato Wedges with this chicken. You'll thank me later.)

Ingredients
- 1 (4 pound) chicken

Spice paste
- 1 tablespoon olive oil
- 1 tablespoon kosher salt
- 1 tablespoon minced fresh oregano

- Zest of 1 a lemon
- Juice of 1/2 a lemon
- 2 cloves garlic, finely minced

1. Rub the chicken

Mix the spice paste ingredients in a small bowl. Rub the chicken with the paste, inside and out. Gently work your fingers between the skin and the breast, then rub some of the spices directly onto the breast meat. Fold the wingtips under the wings and truss the chicken. Skewer the chicken on the rotisserie spit, securing it with the spit forks. Let the chicken rest at room temperature until the grill is ready.

2. Set the grill for indirect high heat

Set up the grill for indirect high heat with the drip pan in the middle of the grill.

3. Rotisserie the chicken

Put the spit on the grill, start the motor spinning, and center the drip pan under the chicken. Close the lid and cook until the chicken reaches 160°F in the thickest part of the breast, about 1 hour.

4. Serve

Remove the chicken from the rotisserie spit and then remove the trussing twine. Be careful — the spit and forks are blazing hot. Let the chicken rest for 15 minutes, then carve and serve.

Middle Eastern Parsley, Coriander, and Cumin Chicken

This chicken's inspiration comes from the Levant, the section of the Eastern Mediterranean stretching from Cyprus and Syria in the North down through Israel and Jordan in the South. (Levant comes from the Latin root for "rises"; back when the Mediterranean was the center of the western world, the sun rose over the Levant.)

The Levant blends parsley, coriander and cumin in their spice pastes. Every cook has their own proportions; here is my favorite, heavy on the coriander and cumin.

Ingredients
- 1 (4 pound) chicken

Spice paste
- 1 tablespoon olive oil

- 1 tablespoon kosher salt
- 2 tablespoons minced fresh parsley
- 1 teaspoon coriander seeds, coarsely ground
- 1 teaspoon cumin seeds, coarsely ground
- 1/2 teaspoon freshly ground black pepper

1. Rub the chicken

Mix the spice paste ingredients in a small bowl. Rub the chicken with the paste, inside and out. Gently work your fingers between the skin and the breast, then rub some of the spices directly onto the breast meat. Fold the wingtips under the wings and truss the chicken. Skewer the chicken on the rotisserie spit, securing it with the spit forks. Let the chicken rest at room temperature until the grill is ready.

2. Set the grill for indirect high heat

Set up the grill for indirect high heat with the drip pan in the middle of the grill.

3. Rotisserie the chicken

Put the spit on the grill, start the motor spinning, and center the drip pan under the chicken. Close the lid and cook until the chicken reaches 160°F in the thickest part of the breast, about 1 hour.

4. Serve

Remove the chicken from the rotisserie spit and then remove the trussing twine. Be careful — the spit and forks are blazing hot. Let the chicken rest for 15 minutes, then carve and serve.

MIDDLE EASTERN PARSLEY, CORIANDER, AND CUMIN CHICKEN

ASIAN BIRDS

We'll continue our world tour with a trip around the Pacific Rim. We'll start in Japan and follow the coast down to Thailand, with many stops along the way.

This chapter's recipes are tied together by soy sauce, the quintessential East Asian ingredient. Earlier in the book I explained why a dry bird is essential for browning. And how marinades don't really work. These recipes contradict both of those statements. (What, you expect me to always be consistent?) Soy sauce is salty enough to work as a brine, has protein in it so it actually helps brown the chicken, and is full of flavor, making it the ideal base for marinades.

Most of the recipes in this chapter are easy to put together from the international aisle of your grocery store. The only ingredients that I have a hard time finding are lemongrass (for the Vietnamese chicken) and gochujang (for the Korean chicken). That said, you should seek out your local Asian market to stock up for these recipes. If you're near a city of any size, you'll find an Asian market tucked away in a strip mall somewhere. I love visiting these stores, and immersing myself in another culture through grocery shopping. And, ingredients are much cheaper at Asian markets. To their customers, these are not exotic gourmet ingredients, they're everyday staples, and priced accordingly.

Most of these marinades have a lot of sugar in them, so I recommend grilling these chickens on medium heat. If your gas grill has an infrared rotisserie burner, start with it at medium, and start checking the chicken after 20 minutes. Turn off the infrared burner when the chicken is nice and browned, and let the chicken finish with the indirect heat supplied by the grill's main burners.

Chinese Hoisin Chicken

If you visit Chinatown, you'll see rows of red, glossy Peking ducks hanging in the windows. Peking duck is an example of Siu Mei cooking — roasting on a rotisserie over an open fire, then glazing with hoisin sauce. Hoisin is Cantonese barbecue sauce, giving Peking duck its distinctive red coating and delicious flavor.

Peking Duck is the best known type of Siu Mei, but it's not the only one. In China, all different kinds of poultry are cooked Siu Mei. This recipe is my take on Siu Mei chicken.

Ingredients
- 1 (4 pound) chicken

Marinade
- 1 cup soy sauce
- 1/4 cup hoisin sauce

- 1 tablespoon toasted sesame Oil

Hoisin glaze
- 1/2 cup hoisin sauce
- 2 tablespoons soy sauce
- 1 teaspoon toasted sesame oil

1. Marinate the chicken
Whisk the marinade ingredients in a bowl until the hoisin dissolves. Put the chicken in a gallon zip top bag and pour the marinade over the bird. Squeeze the air out of the bag, seal, and put the bagged chicken in a baking dish. Refrigerate for at least one hour, preferably four to eight hours, turning occasionally to redistribute the marinade.

2. Truss and spit the chicken
Remove the chicken from the bag and let any excess marinade drip off. Fold the wingtips under the wings and truss the chicken. Skewer the chicken on the rotisserie spit, securing it with the spit forks. Let the chicken rest at room temperature while the grill preheats.

3. Set the grill for indirect medium heat
Set up the grill for indirect medium heat with the drip pan in the middle of the grill.

4. Make the Hoisin glaze
Whisk the hoisin glaze ingredients in a medium bowl. Set aside for later.

5. Rotisserie the chicken
Put the spit on the grill, start the motor spinning, and center the drip pan under the chicken. Close the lid and cook until the chicken reaches 160°F in the thickest part of the breast, about 1 hour and 15 minutes. During the last 15 minutes of cooking, brush the chicken with the hoisin glaze every five minutes.

6. Serve

Remove the chicken from the rotisserie spit and then remove the trussing twine. Be careful — the spit and forks are blazing hot. Brush with one last coat of glaze. Let the chicken rest for 15 minutes, then carve and serve, passing the remaining hoisin glaze at the table for dipping.

Korean Barbecue Chicken

Gochujang, Korean red pepper paste, is the backbone of Korean barbecue. It's a thick, sweet pepper paste, with a blast of heat at the end. (Think of thick, spicy ketchup, and you're on the right track for the flavor.)

Gochujang is showing up in the international aisle of well stocked grocery stores, but you may have to visit your local Asian market to find it. It's worth the effort — it has a bold, sweet, spicy flavor that defines Korean barbecue, and is hard to replace. It is sold in tubs of thick paste, or in bottles of pre-made sauce; I use the tubs of paste in this recipe.

Ingredients
- 1 (4 pound) chicken

Marinade

- 1 cup soy sauce
- 1/4 cup gochujang paste (Korean red pepper paste)
- 1/4 cup pear juice (or apple juice)
- 1/2 cup peanut oil
- 1 teaspoon Toasted Sesame Oil

Korean Barbecue Glaze
- 1/2 cup gochujang paste (Korean red pepper paste)
- 1/4 cup soy sauce
- 1/4 cup mirin (or rice wine vinegar, plus 1 teaspoon sugar)
- 1/4 cup pear juice (or apple juice)
- 2 tablespoons brown sugar
- 2 tablespoons sesame oil

1. Marinate the chicken
Whisk the marinade ingredients in a bowl until the gochujang dissolves. Put the chicken in a gallon zip top bag and pour the marinade over the bird. Squeeze the air out of the bag, seal, and put the bagged chicken in a baking dish. Refrigerate for at least one hour, preferably four to eight hours, turning occasionally to redistribute the marinade.

2. Truss and spit the chicken
Remove the chicken from the bag and let any excess marinade drip off. Fold the wingtips under the wings and truss the chicken. Skewer the chicken on the rotisserie spit, securing it with the spit forks. Let the chicken rest at room temperature until the grill is ready.

3. Set the grill for indirect medium heat
Set up the grill for indirect medium heat with the drip pan in the middle of the grill.

4. Make the Korean barbecue sauce
Whisk the Korean barbecue sauce ingredients in a medium bowl until the gochujang and brown sugar dissolve. Set aside for later.

5. Rotisserie the chicken

Put the spit on the grill, start the motor spinning, and center the drip pan under the chicken. Close the lid and cook until the chicken reaches 160°F in the thickest part of the breast, about 1 hour and 15 minutes. During the last 15 minutes of cooking, brush the chicken with the Korean barbecue sauce every five minutes.

6. Serve

Remove the chicken from the rotisserie spit and then remove the trussing twine. Be careful — the spit and forks are blazing hot. Brush with one last coat of sauce. Let the chicken rest for 15 minutes, then carve and serve, passing the remaining Korean barbecue sauce at the table for dipping.

Japanese Tare Chicken

Japan's Yakitori restaurants are an adventure in chicken grilling. They grill the entire bird, from beak to tail, and serve it on bite sized skewers. You start with white and dark meat, grilled over lump charcoal, dipped in soy-based yakitori tare sauce. Then come the interesting parts — skewers of hearts, liver, gizzards, and skin.

This recipe is a shortcut. Instead of bite sized pieces, I use my spit as the skewer. I baste the chicken with yakitori tare sauce as it spins on the rotisserie spit. (And, don't worry — I'm not expecting you to rotisserie chicken gizzards.)

Ingredients
- 1 (4 pound) chicken
- 1 tablespoon kosher salt
- 1/2 teaspoon Sichimi Togarashi (Japanese ground peppers. Or substitute 1/4 teaspoon crushed red pepper flakes and 1/4

teaspoon fresh ground black pepper)

Yakitori Tare Glaze
- 1/2 cup soy sauce
- 1/2 cup mirin (Japanese sweetened rice wine)
- 1/4 cup sake (Japanese brewed rice wine)
- 1/4 cup chicken broth (or water)
- 1/4 cup sugar
- 1 clove garlic, smashed
- 1 thin slice ginger, smashed

1. Season, truss and spit the chicken
Season the chicken with the salt and Sichimi, inside and out. Gently work your fingers between the skin and the breast, then rub some of the salt directly onto the breast meat. Fold the wingtips under the wings and truss the chicken. Skewer the chicken on the rotisserie spit, securing it with the spit forks. Let the chicken rest at room temperature until the grill is ready.

2. Set the grill for indirect medium heat
Set up the grill for indirect medium heat with the drip pan in the middle of the grill.

3. Make the yakitori tare glaze
Whisk the yakitori tare glaze ingredients in a small saucepan. Bring the sauce to a simmer over medium heat and simmer until the sauce thickens and reduces by half, about ten minutes. Remove from the heat, discard the garlic and ginger, and save the rest of the glaze for later.

4. Rotisserie the chicken
Put the spit on the grill, start the motor spinning, and center the drip pan under the chicken. Close the lid and cook until the chicken reaches 160°F in the thickest part of the breast, about 1 hour and 15 minutes. During the last 15 minutes of cooking, brush the chicken with the yakitori tare glaze every five minutes.

5. Serve

Remove the chicken from the rotisserie spit and then remove the trussing twine. Be careful — the spit and forks are blazing hot. Brush with one last coat of glaze. Let the chicken rest for 15 minutes, then carve and serve, passing the remaining yakitori tare glaze at the table for dipping.

THAI CHICKEN WITH DIPPING SAUCE

This is my take on Thai grilled chicken with dipping sauce, a popular street food in Thailand.

One of the key ingredients in Thai cuisine is fish sauce. Fish sauce is a pungent, fermented sauce, and is used like soy sauce in cooking all over Southeast Asia. It is loaded with umami, and adds a flavor that can't be replaced in Thai cooking...but I go easy on fish sauce in my recipes. If you've never tried fish sauce, be warned — when I say "pungent", I mean "smells like feet". On the other hand, if you love fish sauce (and think I'm a wimp), replace the soy sauce in the recipe with fish sauce.

Ingredients
- 1 (4 pound) chicken

Marinade

- 1/4 cup cilantro, leaves and stems
- 2 cloves garlic, peeled
- 1/2 cup soy sauce
- 2 tablespoons fish sauce
- 1/4 cup brown sugar
- 1 teaspoon ground coriander seed
- 1 teaspoon fresh ground white pepper (or substitute black pepper, or a peppercorn blend)

Dipping sauce
- 1/4 cup lime juice (juice of 2 limes)
- 2 tablespoons soy sauce
- 2 tablespoons fish sauce
- 1 clove garlic, peeled and minced
- 2 tablespoons brown sugar
- 1 tablespoon red pepper flakes
- 1/2 teaspoon fresh ground white pepper (or substitute black pepper, or a peppercorn blend)

Chili sauce
- Bottled Thai sweet chili sauce, like Mae Ploy brand

1. Marinate the chicken
Put the cilantro and garlic in a blender or food processor, and finely mince with one second pulses. Add the rest of the marinade ingredients and blend for 30 seconds. Put the chicken in a gallon zip top bag and pour the marinade over the bird. Squeeze the air out of the bag, seal, and put the bagged chicken in a baking dish. Refrigerate for at least one hour, preferably four to eight hours, turning occasionally to redistribute the marinade.

2. Truss and spit the chicken
Remove the chicken from the bag and let any excess marinade drip off. Fold the wingtips under the wings and truss the chicken. Skewer the chicken on the rotisserie spit, securing it with the spit forks. Let the chicken rest at room temperature while the grill preheats.

3. Set the grill for indirect medium heat
Set up the grill for indirect medium heat with the drip pan in the middle of the grill.

4. Make the dipping sauce
Whisk the dipping sauce ingredients in a 2 quart measuring cup until the brown sugar dissolves. Set aside for later.

5. Rotisserie the chicken
Put the spit on the grill, start the motor spinning, and center the drip pan under the chicken. Close the lid and cook until the chicken reaches 160°F in the thickest part of the breast, about 1 hour and 15 minutes.

6. Serve
Remove the chicken from the rotisserie spit and then remove the trussing twine. Be careful — the spit and forks are blazing hot. Let the chicken rest for 15 minutes. While the chicken rests, pour the dipping sauce and the chile sauce into separate small bowls, one set of bowls per diner. Carve the chicken and serve with the dipping sauce.

VIETNAMESE LEMONGRASS CHICKEN

Vietnamese lemongrass chicken (Ga Nuong Xa) is another street food classic from Southeast Asia.

When you cook with lemongrass, only use the tender heart of the stalk. Trim the root end and cut off all the green leaves from the top of the stalk. This will leave the tight center of the stalk; peel away any outer green layers and what's left is the white heart of the stalk. If lemongrass is not available, substitute a scallion and a tablespoon of lemon juice.

Ingredients
- 1 (4 pound) chicken

Marinade
- 1 (6 inch) stalk lemongrass, root and leaves trimmed, green outer layers peeled away from the heart
- 2 cloves garlic

- 1/2 inch wide piece of ginger
- 1/2 cup soy sauce
- 2 tablespoons fish sauce
- 1/4 cup honey
- 1 teaspoon fresh ground black pepper

1. Marinate the chicken
Put the lemongrass, garlic, and ginger in a blender or food processor, and finely mince with one second pulses. Add the rest of the marinade ingredients and blend for 30 seconds. Put the chicken in a gallon zip top bag and pour the marinade over the bird. Squeeze the air out of the bag, seal, and put the bagged chicken in a baking dish. Refrigerate for at least one hour, preferably four to eight hours, turning occasionally to redistribute the marinade.

2. Truss and spit the chicken
Remove the chicken from the bag and let any excess marinade drip off. Fold the wingtips under the wings and truss the chicken. Skewer the chicken on the rotisserie spit, securing it with the spit forks. Let the chicken rest at room temperature while the grill preheats.

3. Set the grill for indirect medium heat
Set up the grill for indirect medium heat with the drip pan in the middle of the grill.

4. Rotisserie the chicken
Put the spit on the grill, start the motor spinning, and center the drip pan under the chicken. Close the lid and cook until the chicken reaches 160°F in the thickest part of the breast, about 1 hour and 15 minutes.

5. Serve
Remove the chicken from the rotisserie spit and then remove the trussing twine. Be careful — the spit and forks are blazing hot. Let the chicken rest for 15 minutes, carve, and serve.

BUSY BUSY BIRDS

It is time to get complicated. If you have jaded guests, people who think they've seen it all, this is the chapter for you. These recipes are guaranteed to amaze.

Wrapping a chicken with bacon, stuffing it, adding a pineapple to the spit — all the recipes in this chapter take extra effort. Don't worry, you will be rewarded for your hard work. Rotisserie grilling is impressive to begin with — wait until you hear the oohs and aahs as you bring in a spit with a Peruvian chicken, accompanied by multicolored drip pan potatoes.

BACON WRAPPED CHICKEN

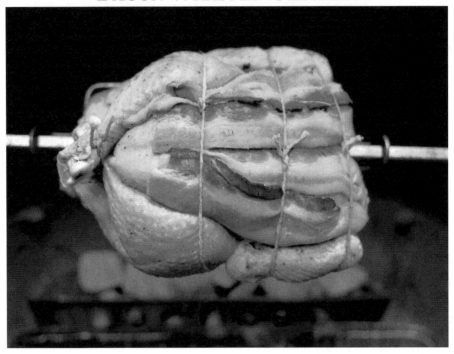

This recipe is inspired by Julia Child's Poulet a la Broche — spit roasted chicken, wrapped with bacon — in Mastering the Art of French Cooking. (That's right - Julia was a rotisserie chicken fan!)

The tricky part of this recipe is tying the bacon to the chicken. If the bacon is flopping around loose, it will burn in the heat of the grill. I truss and spit the chicken as usual — I want it attached to the spit and ready to go. Then I lay the bacon strips on the chicken breast and tie them down, looping around the chicken. I use one piece of twine on each end of the bacon slices, and one across the middle.

After that, everything is easy. Start the rotisserie spinning, cover the grill, and begin cooking the chicken as usual. After 30 minutes, snip the strings holding the bacon, and lift the bacon off of the chicken breast. (The bacon is cooked — it can be a chef's treat, or you can dice it up and mix it with drip pan potatoes.) Finish the chicken — it should take another 30 minutes, giving the skin time to brown — and then it is time to eat.

Ingredients
- 1 (4 pound) roasting chicken
- 1 tablespoon kosher salt
- 1/2 teaspoon fresh ground black pepper
- 2 slices of bacon, cut in half crosswise

1. Dry brine the chicken
Season the chicken with the salt and pepper, inside and out. Gently work your fingers between the skin and the breast, then rub some of the salt and pepper directly onto the breast meat. Refrigerate overnight, or up to 48 hours ahead of time.

2. Truss and spit the chicken, then tie on the bacon
One hour before cooking, remove the chicken from the refrigerator. Fold the wingtips under the wings and truss the chicken. Skewer the chicken on the rotisserie spit, securing it with the spit forks. Lay the slices of bacon on top of the chicken's breast, fanning them out to cover as much of the breast as possible. Using extra butchers twine, tie the bacon down onto the chicken, looping all the way around the bird. Make sure to get the edges of the bacon tied down — any loose ends that flop around will burn. Let the chicken rest at room temperature while the grill preheats.

3. Set the grill for indirect high
Set up the grill for indirect high heat with the drip pan in the middle of the grill.

4. Rotisserie the chicken
Put the spit on the grill, start the motor spinning, and center the drip pan under the chicken. Close the lid, and cook until the bacon renders its fat and is cooked through, about 30 minutes. Cut the twine holding the bacon to the chicken and remove the bacon. (Discard the bacon, dice it up and add it to drip pan potatoes, or eat it as a chef's treat.)

Close the lid and continue to cook the chicken until it reaches 160°F in the thickest part of the breast, about 30 more minutes.

5. Serve
Remove the chicken from the rotisserie spit and then remove the trussing twine. Be careful — the spit and forks are blazing hot. Let the chicken rest for 15 minutes, carve, and serve.

CHICKEN WITH ITALIAN SAUSAGE STUFFING

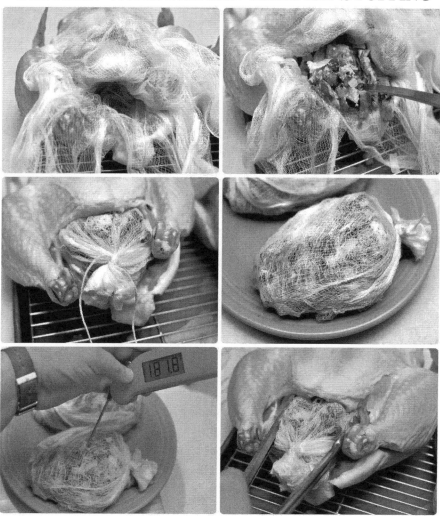

Stuffing a chicken is a tradeoff. It is great for the stuffing, but bad for the chicken. The stuffing comes out moist and full of chicken flavor. But…by the time the stuffing is cooked to 160°F and safe enough to eat, the white meat of the chicken is seriously overcooked.

So, I stayed away from stuffing chicken…until I learned to preheat the stuffing from Kenji Alt in his Food Lab column on SeriousEats.com. Before cooking, line the cavity of the chicken with cheesecloth, stuff the chicken, and tie the end of the cheesecloth shut over the stuffing. Pull the cheesecloth bag of stuffing out of the bird and par-cook it in the microwave. This gives the stuffing has a head start, so it will be done cooking at the same time as the chicken breast.

The only other problem with stuffing a chicken? Chicken cavities are too small, and I like a lot of stuffing. So, I make a big batch of stuffing, way more than I can fit in a single bird. I stuff the chicken as much as I can, then I cook the rest of the stuffing in the drip pan. When everything is done cooking, I stir the extra-moist stuffing from the cavity into the drip pan stuffing. (I also recommend a larger chicken for this recipe — 5 pounds or larger — to get a bigger cavity to fill with stuffing.)

Equipment
- Instant read thermometer (to verify the stuffing temperature)
- 2 aluminum foil drip pans (9"x13"x2" deep)
- 1 foot by 1 foot square piece of cheesecloth
- Butcher's twine

Ingredients
- 1 (5 pound) roasting chicken
- 1 1/4 tablespoons kosher salt
- 1/2 teaspoon fresh ground black pepper

Stuffing
- 4 tablespoons butter (1/2 stick)
- 1 medium onion, diced
- 1 stalk celery, diced
- 1/2 cup dried cranberries
- 2 cloves garlic, crushed
- 1 teaspoons kosher salt
- 1 pound dried bread cubes (look for the bags in the bakery of your local grocery store)
- 1/2 cup minced parsley
- 12 ounces (3/4 pound) bulk Italian sausage

- 2 cups chicken stock
- 1 teaspoon kosher salt
- 1 teaspoon fresh ground black pepper

1. Dry brine the chicken
Season the chicken with the salt and pepper, inside and out. Gently work your fingers between the skin and the breast, then rub some of the salt and pepper directly onto the breast meat. Refrigerate for at least two hours, preferably overnight.

2. Make the stuffing
Melt the butter in a large fry pan over medium-high heat. Add the onion, celery, cranberries, and garlic, then sprinkle with 1 teaspoon of kosher salt. Sauté until the onions are soft, about five minutes. Put the bread and parsley in a large mixing bowl, and scrape the sautéed aromatics from the fry pan into the bowl. Put the pan back over medium-high heat and add the sausage. Cook the sausage, stirring and breaking it up, until it is browned and cooked through, about 10 minutes. Add the sausage to the bowl with the bread and aromatics, and stir until evenly mixed. Pour in the chicken stock, add the salt and pepper, and stir until all the bread is damp.

3. Stuff the chicken
Line the cavity of the chicken with the cheesecloth, then spoon in the stuffing, packing it in as tight as you can. Tie off the end of the cheesecloth and trim any extra cheesecloth or twine. Pull the cheesecloth stuffing pouch out of the chicken, set it on a microwave safe plate, and set aside. Pour the rest of the stuffing into one of the foil pans. Cover the pan with a sheet of aluminum foil, crimp it around the edges to seal, then cut slits in the foil so the chicken drippings can drip through into the stuffing.

4. Set the grill for indirect medium heat
Set up the grill for indirect medium heat (350°F) with grates removed and the second (empty) drip pan in the middle of the grill.

5. Re-stuff, truss, and spit the chicken

While the grill is pre-heating, microwave the stuffing. It is done when it reaches 180°F in its thickest part, about 5 minutes. Use kitchen tongs to push the hot bag of stuffing back into the chicken, and then truss the chicken. Skewer the chicken on the rotisserie spit, forcing the point through the cheesecloth at the center of the bag of stuffing. (Aim the spit just below where you tied the cheesecloth together.) Secure the chicken to the spit with spit forks.

6. Rotisserie the chicken and the stuffing

Put the spit on the grill, start the motor spinning, and center the drip pan under the chicken. Close the lid and cook for 45 minutes. Then, replace the drip pan with the pan full of stuffing, pouring any drippings in the pan onto the sheet of aluminum foil covering the stuffing; it will drip through the slits into the stuffing. Close the lid and cook for another 30 minutes. At that point, remove the foil from the top of the pan of stuffing and check the chicken. The chicken is done when it measures 160°F in the thickest part of the breast; the stuffing is done when it is browned and crispy on top and measures 150°F in its thickest part. Both should take 15 more minutes, for a total cooking time of about one and a half hours.

7. Mix the stuffing, carve the bird, and serve.

Remove the chicken from the rotisserie spit and remove the trussing twine. Be careful — the spit and forks are blazing hot. Carefully remove the pan of stuffing from the grill. Pull the bag of stuffing out of the chicken. Cut the bag open, dump it in the pan with the rest of the stuffing, and toss to combine. Let the chicken rest for 15 minutes. Carve the chicken, put the stuffing on a serving platter, and serve.

Notes

- You need a really big bowl for step 2; if your bowl is overflowing, start with half the bread cubes, the onion/chestnut aromatics, and half the stock. Stir and the bread will shrink as it absorbs the stock; once it shrinks enough, add the rest of the stuffing.

- I usually cook two chickens when I make this recipe — I make one batch of stuffing, stuff them both, then use an extra drip pan under the second bird, which I use to make a batch of drip pan potatoes.
- I buy bags of dried bread cubes from the bakery in my local grocery store. I try to find a bag with a few different loaves in it — white, wheat, and pumpernickel. Around the holidays, these bags can have cranberry or raisin bread mixed in, which adds even more flavor to the stuffing.

Mexican Achiote Chicken

Achiote paste is the definitive seasoning of the Yucatan in Mexico. Annatto seed is ground into a powder, mixed with spices, and formed into small, sticky bricks sold in Mexican markets. These bricks of achiote paste are thinned with citrus juice and used as a marinade. In the Yucatan, they use sour orange juice; I can't find sour oranges in my neck of the woods, so I use a trick from Rick Bayless and mix orange and lime juice to simulate the sour orange flavor.

Annatto seed is also used as a food safe dye; be careful when you're using it — it will stain.

In the Yucatan, achiote is used on everything — seafood, pork, and (of course), chicken. It's also used in Mexico City, to marinate tacos al pastor; spit roasted pork on a vertical skewer with a pineapple on top. I'm borrowing that idea, and adding a pineapple to the rotisserie spit with our chicken.

Ingredients
- 1 (4 pound) chicken
- 1 pineapple, topped, peeled, and trimmed

Achiote marinade
- 1.75 ounces of achiote paste (half of a 3.5 ounce package)
- 1/2 cup orange juice (juice of 1 orange)
- 1/2 cup lime juice (juice of 2 limes)
- 1 teaspoon kosher salt

1. Marinate the chicken
Whisk the achiote marinade ingredients until the achiote paste is completely dissolved. (Be careful — achiote will stain clothes. Wear an apron and roll up your sleeves while you work with it.) Put the chicken in a gallon zip top bag and pour the marinade over the bird. Squeeze the air out of the bag, seal, and put the bagged chicken in a baking dish. Refrigerate for four to eight hours, turning occasionally to coat the chicken with the marinade.

2. Trim and spit the pineapple
Cut the top and bottom off the pineapple. Working around the outside of the pineapple, cut the rind off in 1 inch strips, making sure you cut deep enough to remove the eyes. Once the first strip of rind is removed, you can see the eyes in the pineapple; use them as a guide for how deep to cut. Once the pineapple is trimmed, drive the spit through the side of the pineapple, and secure the pineapple to the spit with a single spit fork.

3. Truss and spit the chicken
Remove the chicken from the bag and let any excess marinade drip off. Fold the wingtips under the wings and truss the chicken. Skewer the chicken on the rotisserie spit next to the pineapple, securing it with the spit forks. Let the chicken rest at room temperature until the grill is ready.

4. Set the grill for indirect high heat

Set up the grill for indirect high heat with the drip pan in the middle of the grill.

5. Rotisserie the chicken

Put the spit on the grill, start the motor spinning, and center the drip pan under the chicken. Close the lid and cook until the chicken reaches 160°F in the thickest part of the breast, about 1 hour.

6. Serve

Remove the chicken and the pineapple from the rotisserie spit, and then remove the trussing twine from the chicken. Be careful — the spit and forks are blazing hot. Let the chicken rest for 15 minutes, then carve the chicken, cut the pineapple into 1/2 inch thick slices, and serve.

NOTES

How to trim and spit a pineapple

Peruvian Rotisserie Chicken

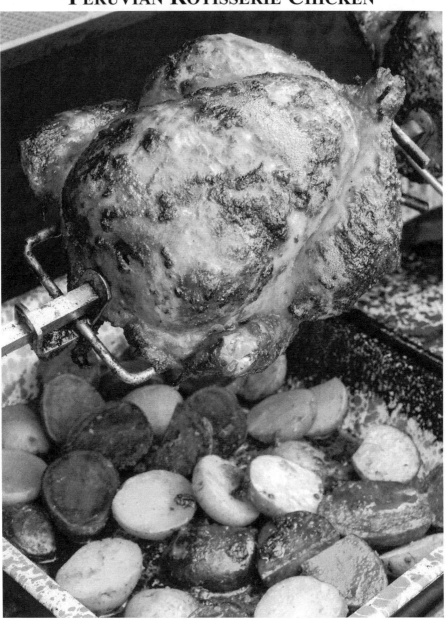

Peruvian chicken is having its moment, with Peruvian rotisserie chicken shops opening up across the United States. Unfortunately, this food trend hasn't made it to Northeastern Ohio, where I live. I finally got a chance to try Peruvian chicken on a visit to wine country in Sonoma Valley.

I talked to the manager at the restaurant, fishing for tips on how to make Peruvian chicken at home. He played his cards close to the vest — all he would say was they had fourteen ingredients in their spice paste, but the one that gave it the distinctive Peruvian flavor was Aji chili peppers. Specifically, Aji Amarillo — yellow Aji peppers.

Back home, I had to order Aji paste on the Internet. Just like the chicken, I can't find it in Northeast Ohio. If you can't get Aji paste at all, substitute a stemmed and seeded jalapeno pepper, which is similar enough to work as a substitute.

To accompany this recipe, I'm jumping the gun on the Potatoes in the Pan chapter. Potatoes are the national dish of Peru, and you really can't have Peruvian rotisserie chicken without crispy potatoes. The first potatoes were cultivated in the Andes Mountains in the south of Peru, where they grew for centuries before spreading across the globe.

I like the way "Peruvian purple potatoes" rolls off the tongue…but a mix of red, white, and purple new potatoes is what I call for in the ingredients. Don't sweat the purple potatoes; different colors of potato all taste the same to me. If you can't find purple potatoes, or can only find one color of new potatoes, go with the potatoes you have on hand.

Ingredients
- 1 (4 pound) whole chicken

Peruvian paste
- 3 cloves garlic, peeled
- 1/2 inch piece ginger, peeled and cut into large chunks
- 2 tablespoons Peruvian aji amarillo pepper paste (or 1 jalapeno, stemmed, seeded and minced)

- 1 tablespoon soy sauce
- 1 tablespoon kosher salt
- 1 teaspoon ground coriander
- 1 teaspoon sweet paprika
- 1 teaspoon fresh ground black pepper
- Juice of 1/2 a lime

Drip pan potatoes
- 1 1/2 pounds new potatoes (A mix of purple, red and white new potatoes), halved
- 1 teaspoon kosher salt
- 1 teaspoon Peruvian aji amarillo pepper paste (optional)

1. Marinate the chicken
Drop the garlic and ginger into a running blender or food processor, and process until minced. Add the rest of the Peruvian paste ingredients and blend into a thick paste. Rub the chicken with the paste, inside and out. Gently work your fingers between the skin and the breast, then rub some of the paste directly onto the breast meat. Put the chicken in a baking dish and refrigerate for at least four hours, up to overnight.

2. Truss and spit the chicken
One hour before cooking, take the chicken out of the refrigerator. Fold the wingtips under the wings and truss the chicken. Skewer the chicken on the rotisserie spit, securing it with the spit forks. Let the chicken rest at room temperature until the grill is ready.

3. Set the grill for indirect high heat
Set up the grill for indirect high heat with the drip pan in the middle of the grill.

4. Prep the potatoes
As soon as the chicken goes on the grill, toss the halved potatoes in a microwave safe bowl with the salt and Peruvian aji paste. Cover the bowl with plastic wrap and microwave until the potatoes are just

tender in the middle. (This takes six minutes in my 1000 watt microwave.) Set the potatoes aside until it is time to add them to the drip pan.

5. Rotisserie the chicken

Put the spit on the grill, start the motor spinning, and center the drip pan under the chicken. Close the lid and cook for 30 minutes. Pour the potatoes into a single layer in the drip pan under the chicken, close the lid again, and until the chicken reaches 160°F in the thickest part of the breast and the potatoes are browned, about 30 more minutes.

6. Serve

Remove the chicken from the rotisserie spit and then remove the trussing twine. Be careful — the spit and forks are blazing hot. Remove the drip pan from the grill and transfer the potatoes to a serving platter with a slotted spoon. Let the chicken rest for 15 minutes, then carve and serve.

POTATOES IN THE PAN

Rotisserie drip pan potatoes are almost as good as the chicken itself. Browned in chicken fat, soaked in chicken drippings, these potatoes are a wonderful side effect of rotisserie chicken.

The trick to drip pan potatoes is par-cooking. Potatoes take a long time to cook. The drip pan, sitting in the bottom of the grill, doesn't get as much heat as the chicken. If we don't par-cook the potatoes, they will be crunchy on the inside when the chicken is done. I par-cook potatoes in the microwave; potatoes cut into small chunks are ready in about six minutes. If you don't have a microwave, par-cook the potatoes in a pot of boiling, salted water. In both cases you want the potatoes cooked most of the way through, but not falling apart.

POTATO PAR-COOKING

Size	Microwave (1000 watt)	Simmering Water
1/2 inch thick slices or cubes	6 minutes	10 minutes
1 inch thick slices or cubes	8 minutes	15 minutes
Halved new potatoes or fingerling potatoes	8 minutes	15 minutes
Whole potatoes	10 minutes	20 minutes

The other key to drip pan potatoes? A drip pan. (I know — thank you, Captain Obvious). Aluminum foil pans are cheap, and cleanup is easy — when you're done cooking, toss the pan. But, even as cheap as they are, I got tired of the expense and the waste, so I bought a 9 by 13 inch enameled steel baking pan. I only use it in the grill, so I don't mind if it turns black around the edges.

Charcoal vs. Gas for drip pan potatoes.
Drip pan potatoes are the one case where gas works better than charcoal for me, particularly if the gas grill has an infrared rotisserie burner. In a charcoal grill, the drip pan sits on the charcoal grate, between the piles of charcoal; heat rises so it is moving away from the pan with the potatoes. In a gas grill, the drip pan sits on the burner covers, above the level of the burners, so more of the heat gets to the pan. Even better, my infrared rotisserie burner points back into the grill, right at the drip pan, making it a great tool for browning potatoes.

If you're working with a charcoal grill, the potatoes need to move around to brown properly. The edge of the pan, right up against the charcoal, gets most of the heat; the middle of the pan doesn't get much heat at all. Stir the potatoes every ten to fifteen minutes with a long handled wooden spoon, to give the potatoes an equal amount of time along the edge of the pan.

In a gas grill, check the potatoes after 15 minutes; if they're not browning evenly, rotate the pan, or give the potatoes a stir.

Finally, try to keep the potatoes to a single layer in the pan. If the pan is overloaded, the potatoes on the bottom won't brown, or cook through.

FINGERLING POTATOES

I learned about drip pan potatoes on a visit to the Sunday market at L'Isle-sur-la-Sorge in Provence, France. The rotisserie chicken vendor fascinated me. One side of his truck flipped open to reveal a wall of spinning rotisserie chickens. Beneath the wall-o-chicken was a sheet of aluminum foil, covered with a layer of sliced potatoes. The golden, brown, and delicious potatoes soaked up the chicken drippings. When you ordered, you got part of the chicken — quarter, half, or whole — and a bag of potatoes sprinkled with salt.

After I came home, it took a few tries to get the recipe right — I learned you had to par-cook the potatoes — and now I can't make chicken without adding potatoes to the drip pan. Chicken without potatoes feels…incomplete, somehow.

Ingredients
- 1 1/2 pounds fingerling potatoes, halved lengthwise

- 1 teaspoon kosher salt
- 2 teaspoons minced fresh tarragon leaves (or 1 teaspoon dried tarragon)

1. Par-cook the potatoes

In the microwave: Toss the potatoes with the salt and tarragon in a microwave safe bowl. Cover the bowl with plastic wrap and microwave until the potatoes are just tender in the middle, 8 minutes in my 1000 watt microwave. Set the potatoes aside until it is time to add them to the drip pan.

On the stovetop: Put the potatoes in a medium sauce pot, cover with cold water, and bring to a boil. Reduce the heat and simmer until the potatoes are just tender in the middle, about 10 minutes. Drain the potatoes in a colander, then transfer them to a bowl, and sprinkle evenly with the salt and tarragon.

2. Finish the potatoes in the drip pan

When the chicken has 30 minutes left to cook, pour the potatoes into the drip pan under the chicken. Use tongs or a wooden spoon to spread the potatoes out into a single layer. Close the lid and cook for 15 minutes, then check the potatoes — stir and toss them if they are browning already; rotate the pan if the browning is uneven. Close the lid and cook until the potatoes are browned and crispy, about 15 more minutes. The potatoes and chicken should be done at about the same time; if the chicken finishes first, remove the chicken to a carving board, and keep cooking the potatoes in the grill while the chicken takes a 15 minute rest before carving.

Spanish Potatoes (Patatas Bravas)

Patatas Bravas are Spain's answer to french fries — cubes of fried potato, sprinkled with salt and smoked Spanish paprika. I borrowed the flavors for drip pan potatoes, with the added bonus of cooking in chicken drippings.

To get even potato cubes, I square off the sides of the potato. Then I cut the potato lengthwise into 1 inch thick planks, cut the planks lengthwise into 1 inch thick batons, and then cut the batons crosswise into 1 inch cubes. (Squaring the potatoes is faster than peeling, makes them easier to cut into cubes, and leaves a little skin on the ends of the potato for added texture.)

Ingredients
- 2 pounds russet potatoes, squared off and cut into 1 inch cubes
- 1 teaspoon kosher salt
- 1 teaspoon paprika (preferably smoked Spanish paprika)

- 1 tablespoon olive oil
- More salt to season the potatoes

1. Par-cook the potatoes
In the Microwave: Toss the potatoes with the salt, paprika, and olive oil in microwave safe bowl. Cover the bowl with plastic wrap and microwave until the potatoes are just tender in the middle, 6 minutes in my 1000 watt microwave. Set the potatoes aside until it is time to add them to the drip pan.

On the stovetop: Put the potatoes in a medium sauce pot, cover with cold water, and bring to a boil. Reduce the heat and simmer until the potatoes are just tender in the middle, about 10 minutes. Drain the potatoes in a colander, then transfer them to a bowl. Sprinkle the potatoes with the salt and paprika, drizzle with the olive oil, and toss to coat.

2. Finish the potatoes in the drip pan
When the chicken has 30 minutes left to cook, pour the potatoes into the drip pan under the chicken. Use tongs or a wooden spoon to spread the potatoes out into a single layer. Close the lid and cook for 15 minutes, then check the potatoes — stir and toss them if they are browning already; rotate the pan if the browning is uneven. Close the lid and cook until the potatoes are browned and crispy, about 15 more minutes. The potatoes and chicken should be done at the same time; if the chicken finishes first, remove the chicken to a carving board, and keep cooking the potatoes in the grill while the chicken takes a 15 minute rest before carving.

HALF BAKED POTATOES

You can cook whole potatoes in the grill — grill baked potatoes are a good thing — but they don't take advantage of rotisserie chicken drippings. That's why I switched to halved potatoes. (That's right, instead of twice baked potatoes, we're making half baked potatoes.)

The potatoes are cooked through, cut in half, and finished in the drip pan. I rough up the cut surface with a fork, creating nooks and crannies that crisp up in the heat of the grill.

Ingredients
- 4 small russet potatoes
- 1 teaspoon kosher salt
- 1/2 teaspoon fresh ground black pepper

1. Par-cook the potatoes
Poke each potato three times with a fork. Microwave the potatoes on

high until they are mostly cooked, 10 minutes in my 1000 watt microwave. (Or, bake in a 400°F oven for 45 minutes.) Let the potatoes cool for a few minutes, then cut each potato in half lengthwise. Rough up the cut surface of the potatoes with a fork, then sprinkle with the salt and ground black pepper. Set the potatoes aside until it is time to add them to the drip pan.

2. Finish the potatoes in the drip pan
When the chicken has 30 minutes left to cook, use long handled tongs to set the potatoes in the drip pan, cut side up. Close the lid and cook for 15 minutes, then check the potatoes and move them around to even out the browning, keeping them cut side up. Close the lid and cook until the rough surface of the potatoes is browned and crispy, about 15 more minutes. The potatoes and chicken should be done at the same time; if the chicken finishes first, remove the chicken to a carving board, and keep cooking the potatoes in the grill while the chicken takes a 15 minute rest before carving.

Yukon Gold Greek Potato Wedges

Browned, crispy, garlicky potato wedges are a side dish staple at Greek diners; I'm moving them into the drip pan.

The obvious pairing with these potatoes is the Greek Oregano, Lemon and Garlic Chicken recipe, but these garlicky wedges of potato go with almost any recipe in this book.

Ingredients
- 2 pounds Yukon gold potatoes
- 1 teaspoon kosher salt
- 4 cloves garlic, minced
- 1 teaspoon minced fresh oregano (or 1/2 teaspoon dried oregano)
- 1 tablespoon olive oil
- Juice of 1/2 a lemon

1. Par-cook the potatoes
Poke each potato three times with a fork. Microwave the potatoes on

high until they are cooked through, 10 minutes in my 1000 watt microwave. (Or, bake in a 400°F oven for 45 minutes.) Let the potatoes cool for a few minutes, then cut each potato lengthwise into 8 wedges. Move the potatoes to a large bowl, sprinkle them with the salt, garlic and oregano, drizzle with the olive oil and lemon, and gently toss to coat. Set aside until it is time to add them to the drip pan.

2. Finish the potatoes in the drip pan
When the chicken has 30 minutes left to cook, put the potatoes in the drip pan, skin side down, using a pair of long handled tongs. Close the lid and cook for 15 minutes, then check the potatoes — stir them if they are browning; rotate the pan if the browning is uneven. Close the lid and cook until the potatoes are browned and crispy, about 15 more minutes. The potatoes and chicken should be done at the same time; if the chicken finishes first, remove the chicken to a carving board, and keep cooking the potatoes in the grill while the chicken takes a 15 minute rest before carving.

SPICY SWEET POTATO CUBES

Sweet potatoes are a delicious variation on drip pan potatoes, thanks to their high natural sugar content. But, be careful — that extra sugar makes them more susceptible to burning than regular potatoes.

I like my sweet potatoes with a hint of heat, so I dust them with ancho chili powder. If you really like hot food, substitute chipotle chile powder and kick it up a few notches.

(BAM!...um, sorry, flashing back to Emeril Live. I'll be OK in a minute.)

Ingredients
- 2 pounds sweet potatoes, cut into 1 inch chunks
- 1 teaspoon kosher salt
- 1 teaspoon ground ancho chile pepper
- 1 tablespoon olive oil

1. Par-cook the sweet potatoes

In the microwave: Put the sweet potatoes in a microwave safe bowl. Sprinkle with the salt and ancho pepper, drizzle with the olive oil, and toss to coat evenly. Cover the bowl with plastic wrap, and microwave on high for 6 minutes. Set aside until it is time to add them to the drip pan.

On the stovetop: Put the sweet potatoes in a medium sauce pot, cover with cold water, and bring to a boil. Reduce the heat and simmer until the sweet potatoes are just tender in the middle, about 10 minutes. Drain the sweet potatoes in a colander, then transfer them to a bowl. Sprinkle the sweet potatoes with the salt and chile powder, drizzle with the olive oil, and toss to coat.

2. Finish the sweet potatoes in the drip pan

When the chicken has 30 minutes left to cook, pour the sweet potatoes into the drip pan under the chicken. Use tongs or a wooden spoon to spread the sweet potatoes out into a single layer. Close the lid and cook for 15 minutes, then check the sweet potatoes — stir and toss them if they are browning already; rotate the pan if the browning is uneven. Close the lid and cook until the sweet potatoes are browned and crispy, about 15 more minutes. The potatoes and chicken should be done at the same time; if the chicken finishes first, remove the chicken to a carving board, and keep cooking the potatoes in the grill while the chicken takes a 15 minute rest before carving.

Drip Pan Beets

Beets are my nemesis.

I don't have many food phobias…except for beets. I can't get the taste of the terrible canned beets of my youth out of my mind.

However, my wife loves beets, and always asks me to make them. I learned that roast beets…well, I can't say that I love them, but roast beets are not that bad. (Especially if you can find Chioggia beets, the Italian beet with red and white rings in the middle.)

Beets take a long time to cook through, and beet juice makes quite a mess. I take care of both issues by microwaving them whole and peeling them after they cool down. This par-cooks the beets, and minimizes the beet juices. (At least, it keeps them from getting everywhere; beet juices will always find a way to make a mess. I think the beets can tell I don't like them.)

Ingredients
- 2 pounds medium beets (4-5 beets, each about the size of a baseball)
- 2 tablespoons water
- 1 teaspoon kosher salt
- 1/4 cup shredded Parmesan cheese

1. Par-cook the beets
Trim the leaves from the beets, leaving a half inch of the green stems attached. Leave the root on the beet if it is still there. Rinse the beets, poke each beet with a knife three times, and then put the beets in a microwave safe bowl. Cover the bowl with plastic wrap and microwave until the beets are just tender in the middle, 11 minutes in my 1000 watt microwave. Remove the bowl from the microwave and let it cool down. (Or, wrap the beets in foil and roast in a 400°F oven for 1 hour.)

2. Peel and dice the beets
When the beets are cool enough to handle, peel the skin with a paper towel — it will slip off with firm pressure. Cut off the root and stem and discard, then dice the beets into rough 1 inch chunks.

3. Finish the beets in the drip pan
When the chicken has 30 minutes left to cook, pour the beets into the drip pan under the chicken and spread into a single layer using tongs or a wooden spoon. Close the lid and cook for 15 minutes, then check the beets — stir and toss them if they are browning already; rotate the pan if the browning is uneven. Close the lid and cook until the beets are browned and crispy, about 15 minutes. The beets and chicken should be done at the same time; if the chicken finishes first, remove the chicken to a carving board, and keep cooking the beets in the grill while the chicken takes a 15 minute rest before carving.

LEFTOVERS

Leftovers are one of those "fight to the death" issues: politics, religion, sex…leftovers. Some people think leftovers are second-rate, and refuse to eat them. These people lack vision. If the idea of leftovers offends you on a deep, visceral level, you might want to skip this chapter. But if you have at least a sliver of space available in your soul for the glory of leftovers, keep reading…maybe I can convert you.

I love leftovers. I never cook one chicken; if I'm going to go through the effort of setting up the rotisserie, I always add a second bird to the spit. I want that extra chicken for later. Leftovers mean I don't have to cook another meal from scratch; they give me something to build on. This chapter shows how I turn leftover chicken into second (or third) meal.

That said, my most common use for leftover chicken isn't really a recipe. When I'm cleaning up the kitchen, I make myself a lunch for the next day. I take any leftover chicken, pull it off the bones, and slice it into 1/2 inch thick strips. Then I take out a 2 cup food storage container, add a scoop of potatoes, and a scoop of vegetables. I fill the rest of the container with sliced chicken and pour any leftover chicken juices from the carving board or platter over everything. I seal the lid, and tomorrow's lunch is ready; two minutes in the microwave at work, and I can grab a fork and dig in.

Another advantage to cooking a whole chicken; Leftovers aren't just the meat. I save the carcass from the chicken and freeze it. When I have two (or more) carcasses, I make chicken stock, the secret weapon of professional kitchens. You haven't had chicken soup until you make it from your own homemade stock.

Don't give up on the leftovers — embrace them!

CHICKEN SALAD SANDWICHES

When I was in the third grade, I went on a baloney and Swiss jag. I ate that sandwich every day, preferably with a yellow mustard smiley face drawn on the baloney. After making my sandwich, mom would work on her lunch; one of her favorites was leftover chicken salad. Mom would shred a cold chicken thigh, stir in some mayonnaise and chopped celery, and her sandwich was ready.

Now I'm the one making chicken salad from leftovers while my kids satisfy their food jags. (They're going through a Nutella sandwich phase.) My chicken salad is a little more complicated than mom's, and I make a bigger batch. I feel good knowing it's in the fridge, ready for me to make lunch.

Ingredients

- 2 cups shredded cooked chicken
- 1/2 cup mayonnaise

- Juice of 1/2 lemon
- 1 teaspoon Dijon mustard
- 1 celery stalk, minced
- 1/2 medium red onion, minced
- 1/4 cup minced fresh parsley
- Salt and pepper to taste

1. Make the salad
Stir all the ingredients in a large bowl until completely mixed. Taste and add salt and pepper as necessary — just enough to brighten the taste of the salad. Serve on toasted bread, or separate a head of Boston Bibb lettuce into individual leaves and use them as lettuce cups.

TACO NIGHT

Taco night is my family's favorite meal. (Frankly, the kids enjoy it more than the original rotisserie chicken.) I put everything on the table, and everyone builds tacos to their own specifications. Kid 1: Cheese and hot sauce. Kid 2: Chicken, cheese, sour cream and shredded lettuce. Kid 3: Everything we've got…but only eat half the taco.

When we have the time, the kids help my wife make fresh corn tortillas from masa harina, Mexican tortilla flour. (Their tortilla assembly line is fine-tuned.) Corn tortillas need to be used the day they're made or they get dry and crumbly. I can't find fresh corn tortillas in my area, even at my local Mexican market; that's why we make our own. If you live in a large city where tortillas are made fresh at a local tortilleria, buy them!

When we're in a hurry, my substitute is store-bought flour tortillas —

unlike corn tortillas, flour tortillas will last for weeks in the refrigerator.

Either way, I shred some leftover chicken, sprinkle it with spices, and sear it in a skillet until it is browned and crispy on the bottom. It's amazing how a little browning changes the chicken from "ugh, leftovers" into everyone's favorite taco filling.

And, while the chicken browns, I buzz up a batch of food processor salsa, and slice a bunch of vegetables. With some strategic store bought ingredients (pickled jalapeños, sour cream, shredded cheese), dinner is on the table in no time.

Ingredients
- 1 tablespoon vegetable oil
- 2 cups shredded cooked chicken
- 1 teaspoon kosher salt
- 1 teaspoon ground ancho chile pepper (or a chili powder blend)
- 1/2 teaspoon garlic powder
- 1/2 teaspoon dried oregano

Food processor salsa (or substitute your favorite jarred brand of salsa)
- 2 cloves garlic, peeled
- 1 jalapeño pepper, stemmed and seeded
- 1/2 cup cilantro leaves and stems (a big handful pulled off the bunch of cilantro)
- 1 medium onion, peeled and quartered
- 1 (15 ounce) can fire roasted diced tomatoes, with juices
- Juice of 1/2 a lime

Toppings and accompaniments (all are optional)
- Flour tortillas
- Shredded lettuce (or shredded cabbage, for more crunch)

- Shredded cheese
- Thin sliced or pickled jalapeños (or both)
- Diced onion
- Sour cream
- Sliced black olives
- Can of black beans, drained and rinsed
- Cilantro leaves, chopped
- Hot sauce
- Lime wedges

1. Brown the chicken
Sprinkle the salt, chile powder, garlic powder, and dried oregano evenly over the shredded chicken, and toss to coat. Heat 1 tablespoon of vegetable oil in a large fry pan over medium-high heat until shimmering, then add the chicken to the pan. Cook the chicken until it is browned and crispy in spots, about 5 minutes. Transfer the chicken to a platter.

2. Heat the tortillas
Put ten tortillas and a damp paper towel in a zip top plastic bag. Microwave on high for 2 minutes. Remove tortillas from the bag and wrap in a clean cloth towel. Repeat with the rest of the tortillas, adding them to the stack in the towel as they come out of the microwave. Let the tortillas warm in the towel for five minutes before serving.

3. Food processor salsa
Drop the garlic cloves through the feed tube into a running food processor and let the processor run until the cloves are completely minced, about 30 seconds. Add the jalapeño pepper and pulse until minced, about four 1 second pulses. Add the cilantro and pulse until minced. Add the onion and pulse until minced.(Don't over-process the onions; they'll turn into onion juice.) Add the can of tomatoes with their juices and run the processor until the salsa is smooth, about 30 seconds. Add the lime juice, pulse once or twice to stir, then taste and add salt if the salsa needs it. (Some brands of canned tomatoes have a

lot of salt and don't need any more; others need some salt at this point. Add salt until the salsa has a hint of sweet, and you can just feel the salt on the tip of your tongue.)

4. Make your own tacos
Put everything on the table and let your diners build their own tacos. Put some chicken in the center of a tortilla, add toppings, squeeze on some lime juice, fold, and eat!

CHICKEN CAESAR SALAD

Caesar Cardini ran restaurants in San Diego in the 1910s until prohibition started in America in 1919. His southern California customers still wanted a drink with dinner, so he opened a restaurant just across the border in Tijuana, Mexico. That's where Caesar invented the dish that gave him immortality: Caesar Cardini's salad.

Caesar salad has turned into a cliché, and the stuff of light lunch nightmares. This is a shame; made properly, it is full of big flavors — crunchy lettuce, garlicky, creamy dressing, and salty parmesan cheese. Add some chicken, serve with a loaf of crusty bread (and a tasty beverage in Caesar's honor), and it is filling enough to be the main course at dinner.

Ingredients
- 2 cups shredded cooked chicken
- Croutons (optional)

- 10 ounces romaine lettuce, chopped

Caesar Salad Dressing
- Juice of 1 lemon (about 2 tablespoons of juice)
- 1/4 teaspoon of sugar
- pinch (1/8 teaspoon) of salt
- 1/4 teaspoon fresh ground black pepper
- 1 medium garlic clove, minced
- 2 tablespoons Extra Virgin Olive Oil
- 1/4 cup mayonnaise
- 1/4 cup grated Parmesan cheese

1. Whisk the dressing
In a large bowl, whisk the lemon juice, sugar, salt, black pepper, and garlic until the salt and sugar dissolve. Add the olive oil, mayonnaise, and grated Parmesan, and whisk until smooth.

2. Toss the salad
Add the chicken, croutons, and romaine lettuce to the bowl. Toss until the lettuce is coated with dressing, then serve.

Notes
- To make grilled croutons: rub 2 thick slices of bread with a cut piece of garlic, brush with olive oil, and grill over direct medium heat until toasted, about 1 minute a side. (Watch the bread like a hawk — it goes from brown to burnt in a heartbeat.) Let the bread cool, then slice into rough 1 inch cubes, and use in the salad

Chicken Stock

Don't throw away that chicken carcass! You haven't used it up yet, no matter how scraggly the bones and scraps look.

Chicken stock is kitchen alchemy, turning trash into gold. Put that carcass in a pot and add an onion and a bay leaf. Cover with water, simmer for 4 hours, and strain out the solids. The result? Stock, the backbone of cooking in professional kitchens. (And now, hopefully, your home kitchen as well.) Stock is essential to chicken soup — you haven't lived until you make soup from your own chicken stock — but it's more than that. Use chicken stock in stew or chili to give it more body, and as the base for heavenly pan sauces.

I make chicken stock whenever I have two chicken carcasses. If I only have one, I seal it in a zip-top bag and freeze it. Then, when I cook my next chicken, I add it to the bag. When I'm ready to make stock, I pull the frozen chicken out of the freezer and drop it in the pot. (Don't worry about frozen bones — they'll thaw as the stock simmers.)

Chicken stock freezes wonderfully, lasting up to six months…but once you find out how amazing stock tastes, it won't last that long.

Ingredients
- 2 chicken carcasses (bones, with any clinging meat and skin)
- 1 medium onion, peeled and trimmed
- 1 carrot, scrubbed or peeled, broken into big pieces (optional)
- 1 stalk celery, cut into pieces (optional)
- 2 bay leaves
- 1 teaspoon kosher salt
- 2 quarts water

1. Cook the stock

Stovetop: Put all the ingredients in a large pot and bring the pot to a simmer over high heat. Don't let it boil; once it starts simmering, turn the heat down to a bare simmer (a bubble or two every second). Simmer, uncovered, for 4 hours.

Oven simmering: Set the oven to 180°F (or 200°F if that's as low as your oven goes). Follow the stovetop instructions; once the stock starts to simmer, move the pot into the oven and cook in the oven, uncovered, for 4 hours.

Pressure cooker: Put everything in the pressure cooker pot, lock the lid, and bring the pressure cooker up to high pressure. Reduce the heat to maintain high pressure, and cook on high pressure for 45 minutes. Turn off the heat and let the pressure come down naturally.

Slow cooker: Put everything in the slow cooker crock. Slow cook on low for 8 hours, or high for 4 hours. (Note — you want the water to cover the other ingredients; if you have a large, wide slow cooker you may have to break up the chicken carcasses so they don't poke up above the water.)

2. Strain the stock

With a slotted spoon, Remove the solids from the pot and discard. Strain the liquid through a fine mesh strainer. Divide the strained stock into storage containers. Use immediately, refrigerate for 2 days, or freeze for up to 6 months.

Notes

- You don't have to wait for two carcasses. If you're in a hurry, you can make a half batch with a single carcass. But, making stock takes long enough that I like to save up the carcasses and do a big batch all at once.

Chicken Vegetable Soup

What should you do with chicken stock? Make chicken soup, of course. Once you have chicken stock in the freezer, soup comes together in no time — it is a quick weeknight dinner just waiting to happen.

Soup is also my excuse to use up leftover chicken; I shred it and add it to the pot with the noodles.

Oh, and a warning: dry noodles suck up a lot of stock. 2 cups of noodles won't look like much when they go in the pot. Don't give into temptation and add more noodles, or the result will be a noodle stew, not a soup.

Ingredients
- 1 tablespoon vegetable oil
- 1 medium onion, peeled and cut into 1/2 inch chunks
- 2 large carrots, peeled and cut into 1/2 inch rounds
- 1 stalk celery, cut into 1/2 inch chunks

- 1 clove garlic, crushed
- 1/2 teaspoon kosher salt
- 2 quarts chicken stock (homemade, from the previous recipe)
- 2 cups leftover chicken, shredded
- 2 cups egg noodles (about 5 ounces)
- 1 cup frozen mixed vegetables
- 1 teaspoon kosher salt
- Salt and pepper to taste (will probably need between 1 teaspoon and 1 tablespoon of kosher salt)

1. Sauté the aromatics
Heat 1 tablespoon vegetable oil in a large sauce pot over medium heat until shimmering. Add the onion, carrot, celery, and garlic, sprinkle with 1/2 teaspoon kosher salt, and sauté until the vegetables are softened and starting to brown around the edges, about 8 minutes.

2. Simmer the soup
Add the chicken stock to the pot, increase the heat to high, bring the stock to a boil, and boil for 1 minute. (If the stock is frozen, that's OK, add the blocks of frozen stock straight to the pot. Cover the pot and wait — they'll be boiling soon enough.) Add the shredded chicken, egg noodles, frozen mixed vegetables, and 1 teaspoon of kosher salt to the pot, and cook for 8 minutes (or follow the suggested cooking time on the noodle package). Taste the soup, and season to taste. The soup will probably need more salt — 1 to 2 more teaspoons of kosher salt — and some black pepper.

Asian Noodle Soup

I serve Asian noodle soup as a "make your own bowl" dinner. I set the pot of hot broth on a trivet in the center of the table, surround it with bowls of add-ins, and let everyone build their own bowl of soup. My wife and I load up on vegetables, the kids make noodle and broth soup, with (maybe) a few shreds of chicken floating in there. (Not that I have any picky kids like that…)

My suggested bowl: put noodles and chicken in the bottom of the bowl. Add some vegetables, and top with shredded scallions, minced herbs, and sliced hot peppers. Ladle hot broth over the top of everything, add soy sauce to taste, and add a splash of vinegar. Then, start slurping.

Use a heavy pot when serving the broth; it keeps the broth warm while it sits on the table. Cast iron is best for this; thick anodized aluminum or stainless clad aluminum pots are also good choices.

Ingredients
Asian broth
- 1 tablespoon vegetable oil
- 3 green onions (scallions), trimmed and cut into 1 inch lengths
- 1 garlic clove, peeled and crushed
- 1 inch piece of ginger, peeled and grated
- 1/2 teaspoon crushed red pepper flakes (optional)
- 2 quarts chicken stock (homemade, from the previous chicken stock recipe)
- 1 tablespoon soy sauce
- Salt and pepper to taste

Add-ins
- 8 ounces vermicelli rice noodles (rice sticks)
- 2 cups leftover chicken, shredded
- 1 pound shredded cabbage (About half a head. Napa cabbage is authentic, purple cabbage looks cool.)
- 8 ounces matchstick carrots
- 3 scallions, trimmed and minced
- Thin-sliced hot peppers
- 1 bunch basil
- 1 handful cilantro (leaves and stems)

Toppings
- Bottle of soy sauce
- Bottle of rice vinegar
- Bottle of Sriracha (or other Asian hot sauce)

1. Sauté the aromatics
Heat 1 tablespoon vegetable oil in a large sauce pot over medium heat until shimmering. Add the green onions, garlic, ginger, and red pepper flakes. Cook for 1 minute, or until you can smell the garlic and ginger.

2. Simmer the broth

Add the chicken stock and soy sauce to the pot, increase the heat to high, bring the stock to a boil, and boil for 1 minute. Reduce the heat and simmer for ten minutes. Taste the broth, and season to taste. The soup will probably need more salt — 1 to 2 more teaspoons of kosher salt — and some black pepper.

3. Prep the add-ins
While the soup is simmering, cook the rice noodles: soak them in hot water for ten minutes, then drain and rinse. Shred the cabbage and carrots, mince the green onions, and slice the hot peppers. Put the noodles in one bowl, the shredded chicken in another, and all the vegetable add-ins on one big platter.

4. Serve yourself
Put the pot of broth on a hot pad on the dining table, surround with the platters and bowls of add-ins, and let your diners build their own bowl of soup.

Notes
- A mandoline slicer makes short work of shredding cabbage and carrots. If you don't own one, and you have good knife skills, you can shred them by hand; otherwise, buy a bags of pre-sliced matchstick carrots and pre-sliced cabbage "for coleslaw" from the grocery store, and skip all the shredding.
- I think of this as a vaguely Thai soup with the thin rice noodles; I use them because they're quick to cook. Don't let that hold you back. From ramen or soba in Japan, to pho in Vietnam, substitute your favorite Asian noodle, and enjoy your soup.

About the Author

Hi! I'm Mike Vrobel, indie cookbook author and food writer at DadCooksDinner.com.

Thank you for reading Rotisserie Chicken Grilling. I had a great time cooking, testing, tweaking, and photographing the book in your hands (or on your e-reader). Frankly, I thought I'd be sick of rotisserie chicken by now, but I plan on making one for Sunday dinner.

If you have a minute, can you please review Rotisserie Chicken Grilling? Online reviews are the lifeblood of independent books like this one. Of course, my ego prefers five star reviews, but any review is helpful.

Enjoyed this book? If you're looking for more rotisserie recipes, check out my Rotisserie Grilling cookbook on Amazon.com.

Comments? Questions? Visit DadCooksDinner.com to contact me. Subscribe to my blog by email for food writing and recipes three times a week; you will also be the first to learn about my upcoming cookbooks.

Thank you for reading!

Mike Vrobel
November 2014

Bibliography and Suggested Reading

Everything I do is built on the shoulders of those who came before me. Here is the food writing that influenced this book:

Rotisserie Recipes

Parsons, Russ. "It's Roasting Outside." *Los Angeles Times*. 16 July 2003.
Purviance, Jamie. *Weber's Big Book of Grilling*. Oxmoor, 2001.
Purviance, Jamie. *Weber's Real Grilling*. Oxmoor, 2005.
Purviance, Jamie. *Weber's Charcoal Grilling*. Oxmoor, 2007.
Purviance, Jamie. *Weber's Way to Grill*. Oxmoor, 2009.
Raichlen, Steven. *How To Grill*. Workman, 2001.
Raichlen, Steven. *Beer Can Chicken*. Workman, 2002.
Raichlen, Steven. *BBQ USA*. Workman, 2003.
Raichlen, Steven. *The Barbecue! Bible*. Workman, 2008.
Raichlen, Steven. *Planet Barbecue!* Workman, 2010.
Steingarten, Jeffrey. "As the Spit Turns." *It Must've Been Something I Ate*. Knopf, 2002.
Vrobel, Mike. *Rotisserie Grilling*. CreateSpace, 2012.

General Cooking Information

Anderson, Pam. *How to Cook Without a Book*. Clarkson Potter, 2000.
Bayless, Rick. *Rick Bayless's Mexican Kitchen*. Scribner, 1996.
Brown, Alton. *Good Eats*. Food Network, 1999-2012.
Hamilton, Melissa and Hirsheimer, Christopher. *Canal House Cooking*. Canal House, 2009-today.
Kimball, Christopher, et al. *Cooks Illustrated Magazine*. Boston Common Press, 1993-today.
Lang, Mike. *AnotherPintPlease.com*, 2006-today. <http://www.anotherpintplease.com/>
Lopez-Alt, J. Kenji. "The Food Lab." *SeriousEats.com*, 2009-today. <http://www.seriouseats.com/the-food-lab>
McGee, Harold. *On Food and Cooking*. Scribner, 2004.
Page, Karen and Dornenburg, Andrew. *The Flavor Bible*. Little, Brown,

2008.
Rodgers, Judy. *The Zuni Cafe Cookbook.* W. W. Norton, 2002.
Ruhlman, Michael. *Ratio.* Scribner, 2009.
Trilling, Susana. *Seasons Of My Heart: A Culinary Journey through Oaxaca, Mexico.* Ballantine, 1999.

Made in the USA
Columbia, SC
25 September 2023